MRS FRAS
THE FATAL

Michael Alexander was educated at Stowe, Sandhurst and Colditz. He has travelled extensively and adventurously in Asia and the Americas, locating 12C Firuzkoh in central Afghanistan and describing the lost minaret of Jham. He was the first person to circumnavigate the north of Scotland in a 4 metre rigid inflatable, and has travelled to the source of the Ganges and through the Great Himalayan Gorge in a small hovercraft. He visited Fraser Island while preparing (with Michael Luke) a film on the subject of this book. He has written a screenplay for Vladimir Nabokov's *Ada* which he is also producing. He is interested in natural history and was a director of *Wildlife* magazine and founder of the Woburn Safari Service. The author of a number of highly acclaimed historical studies, he lives in London.

Also by Michael Alexander

The Privileged Nightmare (with Giles Romilly)
The Reluctant Legionnaire
Offbeat in Asia
The True Blue
Omai: Noble Savage
Queen Victoria's Maharajah (Phoenix Press)
Discovering the New World

MRS FRASER ON THE FATAL SHORE

Michael Alexander

PHOENIX
PRESS

5 UPPER SAINT MARTIN'S LANE
LONDON
WC2H 9EA

A PHOENIX PRESS PAPERBACK

First published in Great Britain
by Michael Joseph in 1971
This paperback edition published in 2001
by Phoenix Press,
a division of The Orion Publishing Group Ltd,
Orion House, 5 Upper St Martin's Lane,
London WC2H 9EA

A CIP catalogue record for this book
is available from the British Library.

Printed and bound in Great Britain by
Butler & Tanner Ltd, Frome and London

ISBN 1 84212 454 4

For Sarah

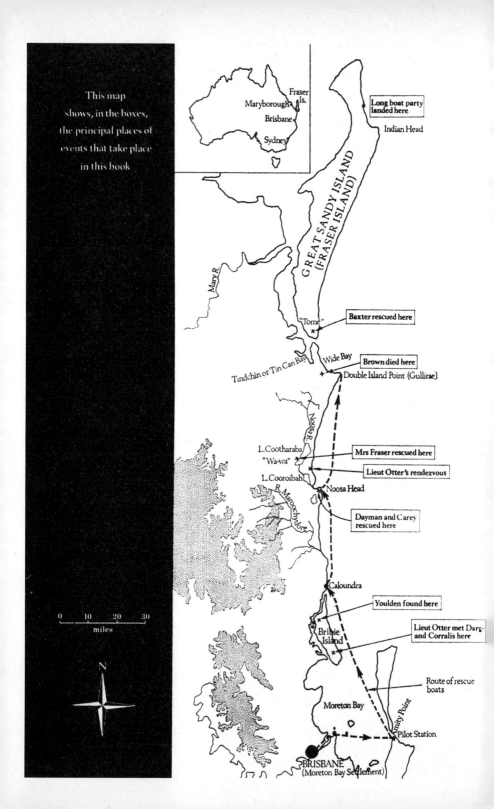

This map shows, in the boxes, the principal places of events that take place in this book

Fraser Is.
Maryborough
Brisbane
Sydney

Long boat party landed here

Indian Head

GREAT SANDY ISLAND (FRASER ISLAND)

Mary R.

"Torne"

Baxter rescued here

Wide Bay

Tindchin or Tin Can Bay

Brown died here

Double Island Point (Gullirae)

Noosa R.

L. Cootharaba

"Wa-wa"

Mrs Fraser rescued here

Lieut Otter's rendezvous

L. Cooroibah

Noosa Head

R. Maroochdore

Dayman and Carey rescued here

Caloundra

Youlden found here

Bribie Island

Lieut Otter met Darg and Corralis here

Route of rescue boats

Moreton Bay

Amity Point

Pilot Station

BRISBANE (Moreton Bay Settlement)

0   10   20   30
miles

N

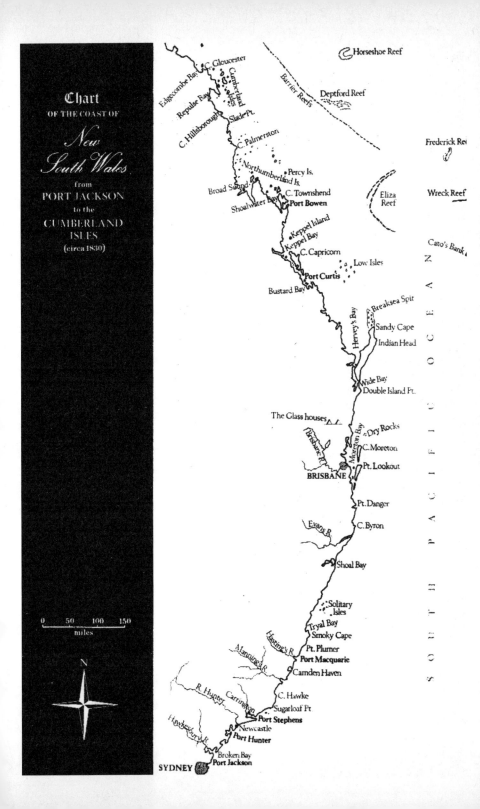

Chart
OF THE COAST OF
New South Wales
from
PORT JACKSON
to the
CUMBERLAND ISLES
(circa 1830)

0   50   100   150
miles

N

SOUTH PACIFIC OCEAN

Horseshoe Reef
Deptford Reef
Barrier Reefs
Frederick Re
Edgecombe Bay
C. Gloucester
Cumberland Isles
Repulse Bay
C. Hillsborough
Slade Pt.
C. Palmerston
Northumberland Is.
Percy Is.
Broad Sound
C. Townshend
Shoalwater Bay
Port Bowen
Wreck Reef
Eliza Reef
Keppel Island
Keppel Bay
C. Capricorn
Port Curtis
Low Isles
Cato's Bank
Bustard Bay
Hervey's Bay
Breaksea Spit
Sandy Cape
Indian Head
Wide Bay
Double Island Pt.
The Glass houses
Brisbane R.
Moreton Bay
Dry Rocks
C. Moreton
Pt. Lookout
BRISBANE
Pt. Danger
Evans R.
C. Byron
Shoal Bay
Solitary Isles
Tryal Bay
Smoky Cape
Hastings R.
Pt. Plumer
Manning R.
Port Macquarie
Camden Haven
R. Hunter
Carrington
C. Hawke
Sugarloaf Pt.
Port Stephens
Hawkesbury R.
Newcastle
Port Hunter
Broken Bay
SYDNEY
Port Jackson

Acknowledgements

My thanks to Michael Luke, writer and film producer, whose longtime interest in the story of Mrs Fraser greatly encouraged me to write this book.

Thanks are also due to Miss Cara Farnes; Miss Anne Dewar; Miss Ingrid Seward; Sir Raphael Cilento Kt.; Clem Lack Esq.; K. R. Mason Esq.; the Rev. Gregor MacGregor; Sir Reginald Barnewall, Bt. and Lady Barnewall (at whose luxurious establishment on Fraser Island I spent an interesting week).

The following Librarians were especially helpful in my researches: Miss Suzanne Mourot, The Library of New South Wales; K. A. R. Horne Esq., The State Library of Victoria; T. A. Kealy Esq., The State Library of Victoria; G. D. Richardson Esq., The Mitchell Library; J. L. Stapleton Esq., The Public Library of Queensland; H. L. White Esq., The National Library of Australia, Canberra.

Thanks also to Fraser descendants now living in New Zealand who provided useful information: Mrs M. Gumbley, Mrs J. Dodds, Mrs E. Shepherd, W. E. Chisholm Esq., and J. B. Laing Esq.

Finally I must express my gratitude to the National Library of Australia for permission to use photographs, in which they hold the copyright, in the following illustrations: The Rex Nan Kivell Collection: 1, 2, 4, 5, 7, 8, 11, 12, 13 and 15. The J. A. Ferguson Collection, 10.

Contents

CONTENTS

Illustrations

WRECK OF THE STIRLING CASTLE

Horrib Treatment of The Crew by Savages

A COPY OF MOURNFUL VERSES

Ye mariners and landsmen all,
Pray list while I relate,
The wreck of the Stirling Castle
And the crew's sad dismal fate.
In an open boat upon the waves,
Where billows loud did roar,
And the savage treatment they
    receiv'd
When drove on a foreign shore.

The Stirling Castle on May 16th
From Sydney she set sail,
The crew consisting of twenty,
With a sweet and pleasant gale.
Likewise Captain Fraser of the
    ship,
On board he had his wife,
And now, how dreadful for to tell,
The sacrifice of human life.

13

Part of the crew got in one boat,
Thinking their lives to save,
But in a moment they were dash'd
Beneath the foaming waves
And Mrs Fraser in another boat,
Far advanc'd in pregnant state,
Gave birth unto a lovely babe.
How shocking to relate.

And when they reach'd THE FATAL SHORE,
It's name is call'd Wide Bay,
The savages soon them espied,
Rush'd down and siez'd their prey,
And bore their victims in the boat,
Into their savage den,
To describe the feelings of those poor souls
Is past the art of man.

This female still was doom'd to see,
A deed more dark and drear,
Her husband pierc'd was to the heart,
By a savage with his spear.
She flew unto his dying frame,
And the spear she did pull out,
And like a frantic maniac,
Distracted flew about.

The chief mate too they did despatch,
By cutting off his head,
And plac'd on one of their canoes
All for a figure head.
Also, a fine young man they bound,
And burnt without a dread,
With a slow fire at his feet at first
So up unto his head.

When you read the tortures I went thro'
'Twill grieve your hearts full sore,
But now, thank HEAVEN, I am returned
Unto my native shore.
I always shall remember,
And my prayers will ever be,
For the safety of both age and sex,
Who sail on the raging sea.

A broadsheet of the period, hawked in the city streets, sets out this gloomy ballad, no doubt composed by such a poet-cum-tinsmith as Mayhew describes in "London Labour and the London Poor". Published in 1837 by J. Catnach of Seven Dials, it is crudely embellished with a woodblock, or "cut", purporting to illustrate its sadistic theme—THE WRECK OF THE STIRLING CASTLE—HORRIB TREATMENT OF THE CREW BY SAVAGES. But the picture, like the beguiling jackets of modern paperbacks, seems to belong to another story altogether—the savages, with embroidered skirts and negroid lips, are more African than Antipodean; the war canoes look Polynesian or Maori; the three-master riding off the palmy shore is not a brig like the *Stirling Castle*, nor is she wrecked upon a reef; the severed heads of women, children and babes in arms cannot have belonged to her survivors, for there was only one woman among them and she had lost her baby before she landed.

The "mournful verses", as the ballad is superscribed, are expanded into a lurid text, which gives yet another version of a much misconstrued tale—three books on the subject were published at the time, sometimes as free with facts as they were with pious rhetoric. With the passing of time the story of Mrs Fraser and her convict deliverer have become more legend than history, and it is not always easy to separate fact from fantasy. Mrs Fraser herself was not the most consistent witness, but with the help of the archives of Australia and London, the contemporary press, books, letters, reports, depositions, and statements, the basic facts of the story can be selected to produce a fair idea of what actually happened. There are areas of question, contradiction and contention but, as far as it is possible to reconstruct from the available material, this is the true unembroidered tale.

"Ye mariners and landsmen all, Pray list while I relate". . . .

I

A Journey To The Antipodes

On Thursday the 22nd of October 1835, two years before the accession of Queen Victoria, the sailing vessel *Stirling Castle* cleared the Port of London bound for Hobart, Van Diemen's Land (now known as Tasmania), and Sydney, New South Wales. A brig of 350 tons, built six years earlier in Merrimac, Mass., and owned by Kerr and Co., she carried several passengers and an unsophisticated cargo shown on her manifest as 5 puncheons of rum, 66 cases and ten casks of wine, 50 casks of vinegar, 300 hogsheads and 52 cases of Hodgson's Pale Ale, 25 casks of mustard, 2 millstones, 22 cases of pickles, 120 tons of salt, 723 deal planks, and 8 cases of merchandise classified as "hard and soft" goods—lesser articles of luxury calculated to appeal to rugged settlers in a junior colonial outpost.

Her captain was James Fraser, of Stromness in the Orkneys. Aged 54, he had made the journey to the Antipodes before, the last time aboard the brigantine *Comet*, wrecked in the Torres Strait in 1830. The only loss of life on that occasion had been two lambs, a cat and a parrot, subject of some bathetic verses he composed in an open boat and addressed to his wife, Eliza (Appendix I).

Shipwrecks were frequent in those days and contemporary reading matter is full of dramatic stories and verses of maritime catastrophe. Such considerations, however, had not deterred his wife from abandoning their three children James (11), David (6), and Jane (15) to the care of the local minister and joining the ship as a passenger, though she might have been further excused on the grounds that at the age of 37 she was in the early stages of another pregnancy. But Captain Fraser, who suffered from a stomach ulcer, was in a poor state of health and nerves, and she was persuaded that her duty lay with him rather than in the home. A contemporary drawing of her, bonneted and shawled, shows a handsome dark-haired lady whose strong features and mobile mouth suggest contradiction between duty and indulgence —an indication that she may also have been anxious to escape the gloomy frigidity of another Orkney winter which, for a lady reared in Ceylon, must have been a positively hostile environment.

Superstitious seamen used to maintain that should an accident happen to an outward-bound ship on the day of leaving port, it presaged a hazardous and possibly disastrous voyage. The *Stirling Castle* made an unlucky start: heading down river past the Isle of Dogs, she rammed a lesser craft and, to quote the report, had her "larboard cat-head carried away". If ominous, this was only minor damage—the cat-head being the boom over which the anchor was raised and lowered—and the apprehensions of the passengers and surly comments of the crew were soon mollified by the reassurances of the captain, backed by his wife's ability to act as if nothing were untoward even in the most contrary circumstances. General anxiety had given way to contented relaxation as the ship safely "crossed the line" and entered the calmer waters of the southern ocean.

The *Stirling Castle* was not the vessel to brave Cape Horn. She took the usual route to Buenos Aires and back across the South Atlantic on the Trades. After a five month voyage via the Cape of Good Hope—in 1799 the merchantman *Albion* had taken three months and fifteen days—she reached Van Diemen's Land with all except her captain in good health and reasonable spirits. Hobart Town, then a settlement of only 10,000, absorbed the vinegar and 52 cases of the Pale Ale, but the bulk of the goods were consigned to Sydney, a thousand miles or so to the north. Several other passengers joined the ship and after a few days' sailing she entered Sydney Harbour and anchored in the Cove, where the owners' agent, Mr Bryant, came aboard to make arrangements for unloading the cargo, urgently awaited by the merchants of the city for profitable resale to the public.

Sydney, capital of New South Wales, had been founded barely fifty years earlier as the main base for British lawbreakers under sentence of transportation. Its main purpose was to absorb the prison overflow once exported to the lost American colony. At the time of the *Stirling Castle*'s arrival, the convict population of New South Wales was 27,000 out of a total of 77,000; every class and category of felon was represented, from "gentlemen" like Sir Henry Browne Hayes—an eccentric Irishman who had abducted a local heiress—to common thieves, highwaymen, pickpockets, forgers, poisoners and poachers. "Political" prisoners included Irish rebels from the Rising of 1798, and assorted rick-burners and machine-breakers such as "Luddites" and "Tolpuddle Martyrs". Age and sex were no barriers to transportation—young boys and women were well represented on the convict rolls. Many transported prisoners were now "emancipists" or "expirees", living their own lives in the territory, sometimes holding minor government jobs or running shops, public houses or small farms. Others had qualified by good behaviour for a "ticket of leave", which permitted them to work on their own account under a system of probation. Unless convicted of further crimes, few were held in prison: at a time when labour was at a premium the majority were "assigned" to settlers or employed on construction work for the government.

The roughness that had characterised the town in its earlier days had been diluted by boatloads of legitimate immigrants. On an earlier voyage (1831), the *Stirling Castle* had brought out fifty-nine stone-masons and their families to build the Presbyterian College projected by the turbulent Reverend Doctor John Dunmore Lang. There was also a large number of girls from English orphanages, supposedly screened by an Emigration Committee in London as being suitable material for maid-servants to the more respectable settlers and military, and sent over on free

Female Emigration

TO

AUSTRALIA.

COMMITTEE:

EDWARD FORSTER, Esq. *Chairman.*
SAMUEL HOARE, Esq.
JOHN TAYLOR, Esq.
THOMAS LEWIN, Esq.
S. H. STERRY, Esq.

CHARLES HOLTE BRACEBRIDGE, Esq.
JOHN S. REYNOLDS, Esq.
JOHN PIRIE, Esq.
CAPEL CURE, Esq.
WILLIAM CRAWFORD, Esq.

CHARLES LUSHINGTON, Esq.
JOHN ABEL SMITH, Esq. M.P.
GEORGE LONG, Esq.
COLONEL PHIPPS,
NADIR BAXTER, Esq.
CAPTAIN DANIEL PRING, R.N

The Committee for promoting the Emigration

OF

Single Women

To AUSTRALIA, acting under the Sanction of His Majesty's Secretary of State for the Colonies, HEREBY GIVE NOTICE, That

THE SPLENDID TEAK-BUILT SHIP

" *David Scott*," of 773 Tons Register,

Carrying an experienced Surgeon, and a respectable Person and his Wife as Superintendents to secure the Comfort and Protection of the Emigrants during the Voyage, will sail from

GRAVESEND

On Thursday 10th of July next,

(Beyond which day she will on no account be detained) direct for

SYDNEY.

Single Women and Widows of good Character, from 15 to 30 Years of Age, desirous of bettering their Condition by Emigrating to that healthy and highly prosperous Colony, where the number of Females compared with the entire Population is greatly deficient, and where consequently from the great demand for Servants, and other Female Employments, the Wages are comparatively high, may obtain a Passage

On payment of FIVE POUNDS only.

Those who are unable to raise even that Sum here, may, when approved by the Committee, go *without any Money Payment whatever,* as their Notes of Hand will be taken, payable in the Colony within a reasonable time after their arrival, when they have acquired the means to do so: in both cases the Parties will have the advantage of the **Government Grant** in aid of their Passage.

The Females who proceed by this Conveyance will be taken care of on their first Landing at Sydney. They will find there a List of the various Situations to be obtained, and of the Wages offered, and will be perfectly free to make their own Election; they will not be bound to any person, or subjected to any restraint, but will be, to all intents and purposes, perfectly free to act and decide for themselves.

Females in the Country who may desire to avail themselves of the important advantages thus offered them, should apply by Letter to " The Emigration Committee, London," under Cover addressed to " The UNDER SECRETARY OF STATE, COLONIAL DEPARTMENT, LONDON." It will be necessary that the Application be accompanied by a Certificate of Character from the Resident Minister of the Parish, or from some other respectable persons to whom the Applicant may be known; but the Certificate of the Resident Minister is in all cases most desirable. Such Females as may find it expedient may, when approved by the Committee as fit persons to go by this Conveyance, be boarded temporarily in London, prior to Embarkation, on Payment of 7s. per Week.

☞ All Applications made under cover in the foregoing manner, or personally, will receive early Answers, and all necessary Information, by applying to

JOHN MARSHALL, Agent to the Committee, 26, Birchin Lane, Cornhill, London.

EDWARD FORSTER, *Chairman.*

NOTE.—The Committee have the satisfaction to state that of 217 Females who went out by the " Bussorah Merchant," 180 obtained good Situations within Three Days of their Landing, and the remainder were all well placed within a few Days, under the advice of a Ladies' Committee, formed in the Colony expressly to aid the Females on their arrival.

LONDON, 1st May, 1834.

By Authority:
PRINTED BY JOSEPH HARTNELL, ... T STREET, FOR HIS MAJESTY'S STATIONERY OFFICE

or assisted passage. A number of these had taken up necessary duties as prostitutes. Two hundred and twenty "single women" had recently arrived on the *David Scott*, whose crew had stated their determination "not to allow the women to be interfered with in any way whatever", by which they meant that their officers should not interfere with access to them on the voyage. "Abandoned and outrageous conduct", the surgeon-superintendent in charge had reported, "kept the ship in a continual state of alarm during the whole passage."

But Sydney was still rough. In a report made the previous year to the Committee of the Legislative Council on Police and Gaols, Colonel Wilson, police magistrate, had commented sternly: "It now covers an area of more than two thousand acres and contains a population probably of twenty thousand souls. This population includes a great proportion of prisoners of the Crown of both sexes; persons whose passions are violent, and who have not been accustomed to control, and yet for the most part have no lawful means of gratifying them. It includes a great number of incorrigibly bad characters who, on obtaining their freedom, will not apply themselves to any honest mode of obtaining a living, but endeavour to support themselves in idleness and debauchery, by plunder, but cannot be drawn from their haunts by the same process that vagabonds are disposed of at home. I believe it will be unnecessary for me to express my opinion, that there is more immorality in Sydney than in any other English town of the same population in his Majesty's dominions. The drunkenness, idleness, and carelessness of a great portion of the inhabitants afford innumerable opportunities and temptations by day and night to those who choose to live by plunder."

Despite these negative factors, the settlement had developed into an expanding commercial community sited on what the first governor, Arthur Phillip, had described as "the most beautiful harbour in the world". Two months before the arrival of the *Stirling Castle*, Darwin had sailed in aboard the *Beagle* and declared himself astounded by the size of the town and the general air of prosperity. There were banks and emporiums, breweries and distilleries, a race-course, a theatre, and several academies for the education of young ladies. If the robustly neo-classic public buildings, dominated by the three-storey block at Hyde Park designed to house 600 felons, lacked architectural refinement, they had a simple grandeur.* The hotels and inns, grog-shops and shebeens were said to be excellent and were certainly numerous—in that year there were 224 licensed public houses in Sydney, and the "sly" grog-shops, as the unlicensed establishments were known, were as available as "speakeasies" during American Prohibition. With churches of five denominations, some nicely-spaced windmills, and lines of terraced houses rising on all sides above the magnificent harbour, the prospect was pleasing and belied the difficulties that had faced the battered survivors of the First and Second Convict Fleets.

The Cove was a busy scene. When the *Stirling Castle* was in port, 47 other ships lay round her, from merchantmen bound for England and the East, to whalers and sealers from North America and Antarctica. Just arrived from Cork with a cargo of convicts was the old *Surrey*, famous for her busty figure-head of Minerva, fully square-rigged, carrying fourteen guns against pirates, hostile natives and mutinous prisoners. No doubt the Captain met a number of sea-going friends and Mrs Fraser visited ashore to give the latest news of London to such local worthies as Mr and Mrs Slade, the Dukes, and Mrs Vitie, taking tea in their parlours and generally recreating the genteel atmosphere of "home". At the Royal Opera House, a grandiose name applied to a large room at the Royal Hotel on George Street, the Frasers saw the great Mr Knowles as that Australian anathema Sir Bumpkin Pedigree in the farce *The First of April or the Inn at Dover*.

* Some of the best buildings, including the barracks at Hyde Park, were designed by the convict Francis Howard Greenaway, transported in 1816 for forging an endorsement on a building contract. It has been said of his work "with the barest means, and in economy in execution he produced architecture that has never been excelled in any land, giving the simplest structures a monumental scale, beautiful proportions and delightfully textured walls."

Like a number of other visiting masters, Fraser inserted in the local papers a notice as follows:— THE COMMANDER OF THE BRIG STIRLING CASTLE HEREBY CAUTIONS THE PUBLIC AGAINST GIVING CREDIT TO ANY OF HIS CREW, AS HE WILL NOT BE ANSWERABLE TO ANY OF THEIR DEBTS. This was a normal precaution, but his crew in fact seemed abnormally unreliable, for the entire company, except for the three officers and a cabin boy who was also the captain's nephew, decided to quit the ship. They presumably wished to seek their fortune in a new land, but may also have felt that a further stretch at sea with so dyspeptic and unlucky a character as their captain and his bossy and dominating lady was no substitute for the racy goings-on and readily available women in "ticket of leave" and "time-expired" convict society. Of the original crew of fifteen, the four who remained were Charles Brown, the chief officer; John Baxter, the second mate and a kinsman of the captain; Edward Stone, boatswain; and thirteen year old John Fraser, the captain's nephew, the only one of the three original "boys" to stay with the ship. Replacements for the deserters, recruited on the docks of Port Jackson, were Joseph Corralis, a mulatto from South America, steward; John Allan, a negro, cook; Jacob Schofield, carpenter; and seamen Robert ("Big Bob") Darge, Robert ("Middle Bob") Hodge, Michael Denny, Henry Youlden, Robert Dayman, James Major, Michael Doyle, William Elliot and John Copeland; and "boys" Robert ("Little Bob") Carey and John Wilson.

Captain Fraser was glad enough to have acquired a crew, but expressed anxiety at having to sail through dangerous waters, where he himself had met with disaster six years earlier, with men who were not known to him and who did not seem very promising material. But he was encouraged because his chief officer, the worthy and well-tried Brown, and his willing, if inexperienced, kinsman John Baxter, were sailing with him and could take some of the weight off his weakened shoulders. He had now been given orders to proceed to Singapore in ballast and there pick up a cargo for London. At about 1.30 pm on May 13th 1836 the *Stirling Castle* weighed anchor, dropped down to "Pinchgut" Island, (so called because it was then a punishment centre where recalcitrant convicts were kept on extra-short rations), and in less than three hours was passing the precipitous "Heads" and entering the wider waters of the Pacific Ocean.

II

Wrecked On The Great Barrier Reef

At the time of the *Stirling Castle*'s visit, the mainland of Australia, or New Holland as it was then generally known in deference to its putative discoverers, was largely *terra incognita*. Less than seventy years earlier Captain Cook in the *Endeavour* had charted the tricky indentations of the eastern seaboard, leaving Matthew Flinders in the leaky *Norfolk* to fill in most of the gaps. But the enormous interior, except for a fifty-mile radius round the settlements, was unexplored and peopled only by primitive aborigines. Though friendly intercourse had been established with neighbouring tribes, even to the extent that the natives prostituted their women to convicts out on working parties, misunderstandings were unavoidable, especially where usurpation of land was concerned. Missionaries, including a party of German Lutherans brought out in an earlier voyage of the *Stirling Castle*, had failed to make a single convert and, despite the efforts of a well-intentioned government, mutual hostility and killings were a commonplace. On a larger scale, almost the entire indigenous population of Tasmania had by this time been exterminated or removed to languish on an offshore island.

The interior was slowly being opened up: the redoubtable Sturt had recently rowed down the Murray River to the sea; Thomas Mitchell was at that time skirmishing with "blacks", as the aborigines were generally called, on his explorations of the Darling River; but the great expeditions by Grey, Eyre, Leichhardt, Kennedy, Burke and Wills, and other bold and dedicated adventurers, had not yet taken place. In fact the men with the greatest knowledge of what lay beyond the settlements were the doubly-convicted convicts, who, to escape the rigours and exasperations of penal servitude and the frequent laying-on of the cat-o'-nine-tails had absconded, or "run", as was sometimes noted in their records, to the lesser evil of a sinister and inhospitable "bush".

In some cases a limited knowledge of geography was the inspiration for more ambitious escapades: in the early days some of the simpler prisoners thought that China was less than fifty miles away, and it was a popular misconception among the Irish, from whom a considerable number of convicts were recruited, that they had travelled all round the world and were thus returned to their point of departure: the nearby Blue Mountains must be, they thought, the homely hills of Donegal or Mourne! Whatever their reason for "running", most were recaptured by mounted troopers of the New South Wales Corps aided by native trackers or, finding themselves incapable of living off the land, returned like truants to take their minimum fifty lashes on the triangle. The toughest escapees became "bushrangers", terrorising outlying farmers and waylaying travellers on the roads until finally disposed of by the military. A very few, however, had managed to get themselves adopted by aboriginal tribes far from the penal centres and out of range of retribution. These men, "supposed to have perished in the woods" according to their records, had thus acquired a knowledge of the interior and the way of life of its inhabitants that no-one else could rival.

With unexplored country, marauding bushrangers, and unreliable aborigines between them, only the sea linked the coastal settlements, and the only way to reach Moreton Bay, four hundred miles north of Sydney and last station on the eastern coast, was by ship. Established in 1825, Moreton Bay (now Brisbane) was one of several penal centres set up to take in intractable convicts sentenced for further crimes in Australia. The regime was excessively harsh and corporal punishment the accepted method of reformation. The area fifty miles around was closed to settlement and no ship might visit without a permit. Thus, Captain Fraser did not think of putting into port but sailed on northwards, past Bribie Island, up the long island low in the sea known as Macleay's or Great Sandy Island,* past Indian Head, where Captain Cook had observed a band of watchful aborigines, and out into the dangerous waters at the southern extremity of the Great Barrier Reef.

Unlike Cook's *Endeavour*, laboriously reconnoitring a route between the 1,000 mile chain of coral outcrops and the coast, merchant ships like the *Stirling Castle* proceeding northwards, sailed well outside this formidable obstruction, the largest coralite formation in the world. To be on the safe side Captain Fraser steered a course on a longitude 155E, to the west of the dangerous and extensive Swain Reef. Towards midnight on the 21st of May, the wind veered from south to south-east, at which time, Baxter, who was acting as navigator, calculated that they were 250 miles south of the Torres Strait, the narrow channel separating the northernmost tip of Australia from the island of New Guinea. All possible sail was set and the ship ran fast before the wind in a north westerly direction. The next day, by Baxter's reckoning, their position at noon was 24S. 155.22E, which appeared to make them well clear of hazards. Running on for nine hours in apparently open waters Brown, who was officer of the watch, heard the sinister sound of hissing surf on his port quarter and suddenly made out in the misty twilight a white outline shaped like an enormous horseshoe. The confused force of currents was so powerful that the helmsman was unable to keep the ship on course and within seconds the *Stirling Castle* was virtually sucked into the encircling reef now partially revealed by the ebbing tide. With a sound like an enormous amplification of splitting firewood she ran onto coral and lay on her side to the sea, which broke right over her sweeping away the sailor John Copeland and the jolly-boat slung over the

* Now Fraser Island.

stern davits. Captain Fraser, who at this time was having one
of his sick bouts, staggered up from below and began shouting
confused directions to the panic-stricken crew. He ordered them
to close-haul the sails, hoping that the sudden force of the wind
might wrench them free from the shoal. Instead, the vessel turned
on her broadside and became a fixture athwart the reef, a $7\frac{1}{2}$ knot
current streaming through her shattered planking.

Confusion reigned among the untried and ill-disciplined seamen and no order was effectively carried out. To ease her, Baxter
suggested cutting the main rigging, and soon after this was done
a violent surge carried away the mainmast complete with the
foretopmast and all the complicated superstructure of a ship in
full sail. Schofield, the carpenter, hacked the mast away with his
axe and for a moment the *Stirling Castle* righted herself, but the
sea struck again with renewed force and it became clear the ship
must soon break up. Water was pouring into the hold and the
pumps had little effect. In the words of Falconer, romantic
hymner of this and other wrecks:

"For while the vessel through unnumbered chinks,
Above, below, th'invading water drinks,
Sounding her depth, they eyed the wetted scale,
And lo! the leaks o'er all their powers prevail!"

By first light the tide had ebbed so strongly that the ship was
high and dry on the uncharted reef and it was now possible to
launch the boats. During the worst of the crisis Mrs Fraser had
behaved with great coolness. When the confusion was at its height
she had gone in search of her young nephew and finally found
him in the lavatory. He was kneeling on the floor audibly implor-
ing the forgiveness and mercy of God to all those who, like
himself, were presumably about to perish in the deep. The
following dialogue, from Mrs Fraser's recollection, then took
place:—

John: "Aunt, are you prepared for death?"
Mrs F: "John, I am afraid I am *not* prepared for death!"

John: "Pray, Aunt, pray—that's the only way! God will
   have mercy on us!"
Mrs F: "John, how do you feel yourself? Do you think
   you are ready?"
John: "I hope so. The Lord's will be done!"

Master John would have been better employed on deck than
down on his knees in the heads; frantic and unco-ordinated
efforts were being made to provision and launch the boats; the
cargo was shifting about in the hold and the crew, headed by
Darge and Youlden, whose one object was to get away in the
boats as quickly as possible, refused to go below to bring up the
water-casks and barrels of salt beef and pork that would have
provided staple provisions for a long voyage. The list of stores
ultimately loaded into the long-boat was by no means ideal for
such a journey as might lie ahead of them:—A clothes bag
containing 50 pounds of bread; three pieces of salt beef weighing
5 pounds each; 20 pounds of pork; 3 gallons of brandy; a small
jar of butter; half a jar of tripe; part of an 18 gallon cask of
Hodgson's Pale Ale; some clothes belonging to the captain; three
trunks of Mrs Fraser's clothes; the captain's sea-chest; two sex-
tants; 2 chronometers; 2 muskets; 1 fowling piece; a brace of
pistols; and an axe. Mrs Fraser was careful to see that a box of
jellies and jams was included for her husband's delicate stomach.
Such solicitude and the fact that three boxes of her clothes were
taken aboard at the expense of more necessary articles may have
contributed to the antagonism some of the crew exhibited towards
her at a later date.

There remained two boats on the *Stirling Castle*—an 18 foot
pinnace and the slightly larger long-boat, both fitted with oars
and sail. Lowering the long-boat proved difficult and no sooner
was it over the side than it was stove on the coral reef, now
revealed by the rapidly ebbing tide to fall like a vertical wall
into the depths of the ocean. Repairs were made with bits of
leather, pieces of sail and other handy material and the launching

was successfully carried out. Mrs Fraser, a sou'wester jammed resolutely on her head, was first into the long-boat followed by her nervous nephew. She was joined by her husband, Brown, Corralis, Major, Allan, Doyle, Darge, Denny and Carey. The pinnace, under Baxter's command, took Stone, Hodge, Dayman, Youlden, Elliot and the boy Wilson. Between 4 and 5 o'clock in the morning of Sunday May 22nd the two boats pushed off independently to clear the surf. The pinnace took the leaky long-boat in tow and they set sail in a south-westerly direction towards the mainland, estimated by Baxter to be about 150 miles away.

The long-boat, towed by the pinnace, did not make an impressive consort. Despite the sailors' efforts at repair she was opening further at the seams and the water entered almost as fast as it could be bailed out. At first they worked in two-hour stints but soon became so weak that they could only keep going for half an hour at a time and then were reduced to twenty consecutive buckets. Finally, they did not even have the strength to lift one bucketful over the gunwale and two men were required to raise a single load. Captain Fraser, despite his wife's earnest tenderings of tripe and jellies, could not bring himself to move at all. Mrs Fraser gamely tried to do his share but on their third day in the boats, inevitably accelerated by her physical effort, she felt the pangs of impending childbirth and collapsed into the scuppers. Her position was such that the baby emerged under water, and though it actually lived for a few seconds, can literally be said to have been "born drowned". The sympathetic Brown tore off a piece of his shirt and wrapped it around the unfortunate infant, which he gently consigned to the sea, where no doubt it was soon taken by one of the many sharks that cruised the reef. This unhappy incident had less effect on her than might be supposed and she later said that she was hardly aware that it had happened.

On the fifth day in the open boats the despondent company reached a small island, which Baxter identified as one of the Cumberland group. Though far from the mainland and well to the north of the reef on which they had been wrecked, it would serve as a base for repairs and rehabilitation and put them in better order to make the journey to the nearest settlement, Moreton Bay, some 500 miles to the south. Apart from the condition of the boats and the fact that the prevailing wind and currents were against them, it was by no means an impossible voyage and they would not have forgotten the exploit twenty-five years ago, of Captain Bligh R.N., the unpopular governor of New South Wales, who in his early days at sea in command of *HMS Bounty* had been cast adrift in a boat little larger than theirs and had reached safety after a sail of 3,600 miles. Matthew Flinders also, wrecked in the *Porpoise* on a nearby reef (Wreck Reef), had safely made his way back to Sydney in an open boat.

Their first action after landing on the sandy beach was to light a fire and prepare a meal, in this case four pounds of pork and some biscuit between them. The redoubtable Mrs Fraser was the first to find water, which they had failed to include in their stores and had been drinking the limited amount of ale instead. Despite her recent ordeal, she clambered up a cliff to a seeping fissure and, soaking her sleeve in it, eventually squeezed out a cupful. As she was proudly offering it to her sick husband, Youlden, who during the wreck and throughout the boat-trip had revealed a mean and insubordinate disposition, grabbed the cup and began to drink himself, saying he did not see why the captain should be the only one to have water as well as all the other good things his wife had reserved for him. When Mrs Fraser rounded on him he parted with it angrily, saying, according to her subsequent denunciation: "Damn you, you she-captain, if you say much more I'll drown you!", and no doubt uttering other seaman-like imprecations under his breath, an indication that she had taken over from her husband the leadership he was no longer able to exercise.

Strengthened by their meal, the crew unloaded the boats and made a tent of sails for the captain and his wife. Night had fallen and they stoked up the fire and set a watch against wild beasts and hostile natives. This precaution proved unnecessary as the place was uninhabited, though in fact the island had had other visitors, for Mrs Fraser found a sailor's tin pot with the initials W.T.T. hanging forlornly on a bush. Early next morning the boats were hauled up on to the beach for repairs: an amalgam of sand, soap and grease took the place of regulation pitch and oakum in caulking the seams, and a number of other professional improvisations were employed by the sailors. On the morning of the 29th they set off again, the pinnace towing the long-boat as before. They now headed in the direction of the mainland, with the intention of keeping as near to the coast as possible should the boats become unseaworthy or their provisions run out.

To obtain more water they attempted putting ashore in an area Baxter identified as Repulse Bay. But the wind suddenly changed and the rickety boats were driven back into the main sea. This was the start of a trial that lasted 28 days, during which time they were unable to land, except on small sections of reef exposed at low tide and from which, if the sea permitted, they gathered limpets and other shellfish. These outcrops were at one time so frequent that the sailors had to drag the boats across them, lacerating their feet on the sharp coral and risking treading on the stone-fish whose thirteen poisoned spines could bring a rapid and an excruciatingly painful death. Venomous sea-snakes, black and yellow with bright spots on their flattened tails, were often seen, while above, the vulturine outline of albatross and frigate bird seemed to dog their progress; below, unpleasant implications of underwater activity occasionally revealed themselves—dark-grey sihouettes of shark, or black, flapping stingrays with wings larger than tea-trays.

The water they had collected on the island was soon finished. They were reduced to chewing the damp hops in the bottom of the barrel and emulating the old seamen's trick of sucking a piece of lead. When rain fell they would spread their clothes out to catch it. Mrs Fraser found that drinking sea-water did not make her sick as it did the others; at her encouragement Baxter tried it but became so nauseated that he had to be transferred to the long-boat, which had become a sort of hospital, sick in both structure and content. The newly promoted boatswain, Stone, took command of the healthy pinnace.

Stone, it appears, was a villain. The occupants of the long-boat —Captain and Mrs Fraser, Brown, Baxter, Youlden, Doyle, Corralis, Darge, Denny, Elliot, Dayman and the 17-year-old Carey—now anchored on a large rock to await the return of the pinnace, which had supposedly set off independently to look for water. They waited two long days, searching the horizon and speculating on its fate, until they eventually realised that it would never come back, and that in all probability Stone had intentionally abandoned them. As Baxter, who was not given to exaggeration, was later to put it: "I was taken ill, and obliged to give charge of the pinnace to the boatswain, who no sooner got her in his possession than he ran away from us." Captain Fraser, who was obsessed by cannibals, put forward the more generous theory that they had been taken prisoner and in all probability eaten.

Alone now, the long-boat limped on southwards. For seven days they were entirely without food or water. Captain Fraser became hysterical, screaming and biting his tongue, shouting impossible orders and rambling on about the loss of the *Comet*, the wrath of God and the horrors of cannibalism. But, thanks to his wife's ministrations, he soon returned to a more reasonable frame of mind. At this stage the more experienced members of the crew started talking about "drawing lots", a reference which was understood by all except Mrs Fraser to mean that the unsuccessful drawer would be available as food for the rest. Though seldom described in books, this system of survival was not uncommon among shipwrecked sailors or, indeed, escaping convicts (Appendix II). There was the story of the unlucky seaman who pleaded with his companions not to kill him outright but to start their dinner on his calves. But Captain Fraser would hear nothing of it, arguing that the hand of God would no doubt

33

protect them if they took their chance living on the fruits of the sea, but would certainly smite them if they set up a tabernacle to Moloch. Darge and Youlden insisted that their only hope was to take their chance on land and come upon missionaries (Appendix III), who they quite erroneously thought to be operating in the area. Seeing smoke on the coastline, they threatened to throw the captain overboard unless he brought the boat in. Other members of the crew backed them and they headed towards the shore, which was not in fact the mainland but the northernmost end of Great Sandy Island.

III

Cast Away

Many thousands of years before European navigators first touched *Terra Australis*, aborigines driven from the islands to the north had peopled the continent with their resilient stock, parcelling out the huge territory among tribes and families, living off the land and waters, moving from place to place in search of food, having no agriculture and no domesticated animal except the dog. They lived hard, hunting and fishing and eating almost anything that came to hand. At certain seasons of the year they went hungry.

Physical characteristics and tribal practices varied across the continent, as did their innumerable dialects. Those on the east coast, in the area where Captain Fraser and his party landed, were members of the Kabi tribe. They could not, by European standards, be described as beautiful—flat-nosed and flabby-mouthed, they matted their hair with beeswax into a mop, adding such elegancies as parrot feathers, the front teeth of kangaroos, jaw-bones of fish, pieces of wood and sometimes tails of dogs. Nasal septums were ritually pierced and bits of bone or kangaroo-skin often inserted. Scarification—the crude cutting of the flesh with oyster shell or flint to form scars—was practised on back, chest and arms.*

When going to battle, camouflaging themselves for a hunt,

* The cicatrices were cut in various patterns and degree according to tribal customs, being worn as a sort of family armorial bearing or badge of rank. They were cut into the muscle of back, breast and upper arm, the newly-opened wound being filled with fat and powdered charcoal to keep it open. When healed it had the appearance of two lips. Stinging ants were sometimes applied to raise the weal.

grieving for a deceased friend, taking part in a tribal gathering or *corroboree*, or sometimes for the sake of elegance, they would paint themselves with white pipe-clay or yellow and red ochre applied in streaks over the body according to the taste of the decorator or the symbolism to be conveyed: a circle round the eyes, the skeletonal picking-out of ribs, dotted lines around thighs and legs, and zig-zags up the spine might be a typical exercise in exhibitionism. They had their magic and their mysteries, their songs and sagas, and they created pictures of considerable complexity. Though they might wear a cloak of possum or kangaroo skin in the cold, men and women were generally completely naked except for unmarried girls who wore a strip of bark around the waist. They made fire by friction, using the spearlike flower-stalks of the grass-tree; to avoid the tiresome effort of making new fire to burn the underbrush for game, they carried sticks of slow smouldering wood whenever they were on the move. The people of this area had little experience of white men, though stories must have come through their very efficient "bush" telegraph that they had done them various harm and were in no way to be trusted. In general, however, Europeans who had fallen into their hands had been treated with great kindness.

They were effectively a stone-age people. Their only cutting instruments were made of flint or shell, fastened between a cleft stick with gum and fibre. Their weapons consisted of spears, *boomerangs*, various types of clubs or *waddys*, stone tomahawks and small oblong wooden shields. Spears were generally from seven to ten feet long with the point hardened by fire, sometimes embedded with flints or the jagged tail of the stingray. They could throw them from fifty to sixty feet with great precision, the impetus being greatly increased by the use of the *toomera*, a short throwing stick which hooked to the top of the spear and acted as a sling; this sophisticated device does not, however, seem to have been developed by the primitive Kabi tribe. The *boomerang* was a curved piece of hardwood, thirty or forty inches in length and shaped with great precision to present cunning aerodynamic surfaces when thrown. An expert could hurl it seventy or eighty yards, after which it would make a sharp turn, fly over his head and behind him another forty yards, curve round and gradually descend to his feet. This was for show; the hunting model was not constructed to return; usually it hit the target with infallibility—a flying duck, the leg of a kangaroo, or a rival in battle. Though argumentative, they were not a warlike people and their fights, usually over stolen women, were more demonstrative than lethal.

There is sufficient evidence, some provided by the *Stirling Castle* survivors, that the Australian aborigines were cannibals. Reports may have been exaggerated by missionaries anxious to establish a greater need for salvation in their flock, by settlers attempting to justify the mass-extermination many of them advocated, or by imaginative travellers telling an exciting tale. But if they did not hunt men specifically, like their cousins in New Guinea and Borneo, they were not, it would appear, above eating an enemy, a dead relation or even a superfluous or refractory child, especially at a time when protein was in particular demand. Indeed, this ultimate resource is thought to have saved many groups from extinction. The Rev. Joseph Orton, visiting Australia at the time of this story, interviewed a runaway convict called William Buckley, who had lived with the aborigines for thirty-two years. He learned "an appalling fact, which is too well substantiated, that these barbarous creatures, not satisfied with the practice of infanticide, are cannibals, and that of the grossest and most shocking description. Their wanderings habits render it inconvenient to carry about their young infants, and it is not infrequently the case that when a second child is born before the former is able to walk, one or the other is destroyed or eaten by them." Captain Fraser's ancestors, it might be remembered, were themselves not averse to the taste of human flesh; as late as the 4th century, Gibbon tells us, "a valiant tribe of Caledonia, the Attacotti, are accused by an eyewitness of delighting in the taste of human flesh. When they hunted the woods for prey, it is said that they attacked the shepherd rather than his flock and that they curiously selected the most delicious and brawny parts both of males and females, which they prepared for their horrid repast."

The first sign the *Stirling Castle* party had of the aborigines was an extended *coooo-ee*, long on the first syllable, short and raised on the second, their standard identification call whose precise interpretation depended on its cadence. Heard for the first time it had a sinister quality that startled and made them look apprehensively in the direction of the sound. A group of five natives stood on the top of the high bluff silhouetted against the sky. They carried spears in their hands and, though they took up an arrogant and even aggressive stance, it was apparent that they were agitated and undecided at the sight of the peculiar strangers. They consulted among themselves. Then, as if making a great decision, they advanced warily to the beach, lay down their weapons, and placed an object on the ground a few feet away with apparently friendly gestures of "come and get it".

Captain Fraser had drawn his pistol, but Darge, who had shown himself to be something of a know-all where natives were concerned and had always, in their animated discussions on the subject in the long-boat, expressed confidence in obtaining their friendship if the right method of approach was used, waved him aside and advanced boldly towards the object in the sand, which turned out to be a large piece of decomposing kangaroo. When he returned triumphantly carrying the meat, the natives seemed to think that a bargain had been struck, for without further discussion they rushed on their visitors and seized caps, scarves and other removeable clothing, more, it seemed, by way of reprisal than regular barter. The Captain lost his favourite nautical cap, but Mrs Fraser was able to retain her sou'wester—having grabbed it from her head, they smelt it suspiciously and threw it on the ground in disgust.

The aborigines then retired into the bush with their trophies, soon returning with a party of friends, who uttered excited *coooo-ees* and chattered in high-pitched voices with extreme rapidity and incomprehensibility, but in a manner that somehow conveyed cupidity as well as astonished interest. They were armed with spears and clubs, and this time they did not lay them reassuringly on the ground but brandished them assertively, beckoning the visitors to accompany them into the woods beyond. Darge was for following, but Captain Fraser ordered the party to stay where they were, under the protection of their weapons and with the boat as a means of retreat when it had been repaired. A shot was fired by way of warning and the natives, who had heard all about the miraculous power of firearms,* discreetly withdrew into the trees.

The kangaroo meat was eaten with relish, but they were still too weak from lack of food to drag the boat up on to the beach. Nor did the "bread-fruit" they found growing on the forest edge improve their condition. This was presumably the *pandanus*, or screw-pine, which is found extensively along the island shore; it gave them violent diarrhoea and was described by Doyle as being no more palatable than "the stalk of scotch kale". After four days of this inferior diet they were almost relieved when the natives returned, this time in large numbers, as though the whole tribe had been summoned from some distant place to look at the new arrivals and take advantage of the good things they had brought from the sea.

Commerce rather than retribution seemed to be the purpose of the gathering. The aborigines stood at some distance and one of them opened the market by throwing a large fish into the "no-man's-land" between them. The sailors in their turn threw in some article of clothing as payment and soon they had enough fish—a species of grey mullet—to make a meal. This system of trading continued for some days, the aborigines acquiring almost all their wardrobe, though why they needed clothes was not clear

* E. Armitage of Maryborough, Queensland, has translated aboriginal *corroboree* songs of the area, one of which refers to a boat from Flinders' expedition landing at Wathuba Creek on the north-west coast of Great Sandy Island; their song tells of their intention to welcome the white men, but that they were frightened by the sight and sound of their guns shooting wildfowl.

as, apart from fillets round their brows, they were never seen to wear a single stitch. Darge, who had heard stories from convicts in Sydney, put forward the theory that they were for the use of gangs of bushrangers living in caves in the mountains, and he painted a vivid picture of their violent existence. They had women with them too, he said, to explain the use to which Mrs Fraser's whale-boned dresses and several elegant bonnets might reasonably be applied.

The long-boat had now been pulled up the beach for repairs, and the six-foot water-snake found attached to the bottom turned into an acceptable dinner, which even the Frasers relished despite the local distaste for eel in the Scottish Highlands. It became clear that the heat of the sun had widened the seams, and several additional planks had cracked. The wind was blowing consistently from the south, and even if the boat had been in good order it would have been difficult to make progress in the required direction. It was Captain Fraser's sensible plan to wait for a change of weather, but by the eleventh unfavourable day tempers were rising among the crew at the lack of action. Although the natives had not shown any overt hostility, and despite the need to preserve the restraining factor of their numbers and armoury, disgruntled seamen, emboldened by the last of the brandy, decided they were damned if they were going to hang around much longer. The ringleaders, Darge and Youlden, solemnly swore that if the wind had not shifted by the time the moon had entered its second quarter—a period that usually brought about a change in the weather—they would take their chance with the savages and walk to Moreton Bay, even though it was at least three hundred miles away if they followed the coastline.

The new phase of the moon had no effect whatever on the wind and the sailors insisted on keeping their oath. It was virtually a case of mutiny, but Captain Fraser was too weak to make an issue of it. Brown backed his captain, but was clearly in two minds as to the best course to take. Doyle, despite the efforts of the Darge group to persuade him to join them, elected to remain, as did Corralis, who regarded himself as the Frasers' personal servant and throughout their troubles had given touching examples of loyalty. Taking the captain's fowling piece (which would have been invaluable for shooting birds), Darge, followed by Youlden, Dayman, Denny, Elliot, and Carey, quit their companions and set off defiantly down the endless beach.

IV

Captured By Cannibals

Captain Cook had failed to realise that Great Sandy Island was not part of the mainland. About eighty miles long and at its widest fifteen, it is in fact separated by a difficult channel into which the Mary River discharges its pale grey silt. Proceeding down the seaward shore it would have been necessary for the survivors of the *Stirling Castle* to cross the three-mile-wide channel forming the head of Wide Bay before they gained the mainland proper and, with the exception of some lesser rivers, a clear passage to Moreton Bay. Their first impressions had been favourable—the wide skies piled high with cumulae, the pounding surf, the silver beach, the piny woods, reminded the Frasers of their Orkney shore, even to the familiar oyster-catchers that paraded the sand in pairs. No doubt the sailors pointed to the homely crows that wheeled above them in the breeze. But in his fear of the aborigines Captain Fraser was still determined to quit as soon as possible and make for Moreton Bay by sea.

Now that opposition was reduced from eleven to six, the natives became bolder, the more daring among them gesturing ferociously with their spears and clubs and darting forward to grab property without any attempt at payment in kind. Food was now more dearly purchased: Mrs Fraser's Indian trunk, brought back by her husband from an earlier journey to the East, fetched only two small mullet and some pounded fern-root on the arbitrary exchange. More and more tribesmen appeared on the scene, the atmosphere seemed to be increasingly antagonistic, and the depleted party felt that some sort of attack was imminent. The wind had still not shifted, so it was impossible to put to sea; at Baxter's urging Captain Fraser decided that the best plan after all was to try to reach Moreton Bay like the others, on foot. Under cover of darkness they abandoned their makeshift camp, setting fire to the boat and leaving the stores they could not carry to occupy the future attention of the aborigines for as long as possible. With nine hoarded mullet as their sole reserve of food, the little party crept off down the moonlit strand.

It was a peculiar procession. The captain, a pistol in his belt, limped along on his wife's arm; Brown and Baxter had muskets (which they soon abandoned); Doyle had a pistol; Corralis, the rearguard, carried a huge stick, and each held a fire-brand in the native fashion, made from slow-burning fibres of a pine-tree. Captain Fraser found progress difficult and the weakness of his bowels necessitated frequent stops. Impatient at the delays, Baxter, Corralis and Doyle went on ahead to light a fire and prepare a meal.

After an uneventful walk of several hours, at times hopefully wading in the surf to hide their footprints from possible pursuers, Baxter and his party pitched camp in a gully at the base of the sandy cliffs, made a fire and cooked all the fish, some for supper and the rest as reserve rations. By the time they had finished their meal, there was no sign of the captain's small group. Fearing that something might be amiss, they slept fitfully and maintained a watch. Daylight came and still there was no sign of the stragglers; no footprints save their own were to be seen on the strand. In case their friends had met with disaster during the night, they nervously retraced their route, but before they had gone more than a mile they were startled to see a number of natives advancing down the scree towards them. They tried to hide in the rocks, but the aborigines bore down on them at a run and soon surrounded them. It was not, apparently, a hostile confrontation: as a sign of their pacific intentions, or perhaps in fear of the white man's weapons, the natives placed their spears on the sand, though it was noticed that they surreptitiously dragged them along with their toes as they advanced. Baxter made signs that they were thirsty and to his surprise the aborigines, in the most friendly and enthusiastic manner, demonstrated a way of obtaining water that was quite new to him—it appeared that simply by digging a hole in the sand, fresh water would filter through, which was then cooled and sweetened with a shrub resembling furze.*

Having performed this helpful service, the aborigines showed their familiar propensity for getting the best of a bargain. Spears now in hand, they began to grab the sailors' moveable possessions, hurrying off into the bush like seagulls with a scrap to hide their loot before a rival might take it off them. The next demand was for the clothing off their backs. Baxter, whose uniform coat was decorated with desirable gilt buttons, was the first to be accosted and when he refused to part with it saw a look of intense resentment on their faces, which was followed by an assault with clubs, or *waddies*, on his head. His coat was forcibly removed and further blows inflicted when he tried to hide his greatest treasure—a locket containing some hair of his aunt Mary, who lived near Wapping. His precious sextant, hidden beneath his coat, caused some puzzlement, and they made signs that they wanted a demonstration of its function. Having set it, Baxter placed it in the hands of his questioner, who seeing "Beegie", the sun-spirit, mysteriously directed to his feet, reacted in a mixture of astonishment and alarm and quickly handed it back to its anxious owner. Quadrant, compasses and chronometers were treated with less respect, being broken up and used to decorate the already elaborate headgear of the purloiners.

Doyle was next, and the Irishman stubbornly stood his ground, drawing his pistol and pointing it at his assailants. Instantly a spear was thrust at him, passing through his jacket at the same time as another whizzed immediately over his head—near misses apparently designed to demonstrate the lethal potential of the weapon. Baxter advised Doyle not to resist, but to submit quietly and lay down his pistol. No sooner had he reluctantly done so

* Captain Cook's men had sunk and filled whole barrels by this method.

than, as if in punishment for his temerity, the native warriors stripped him naked. Then, as if tiring of a game, they gave a triumphant *coooo-ee* and ran off into the woods.

A short time later, Baxter spotted Captain Fraser and his little party limping along the sands. They presented a grotesque and melancholy appearance. The captain was bleeding profusely from the cheek. They were all naked; Mrs Fraser, however, had made a modest effort to string around her loins a wreath of the mauve-flowered sea-grape that trailed everywhere across the sandhills, secreting her wedding ring and earrings among the tendrils. The story they had to tell was dramatic: shortly after separating they had been followed by the same natives who had been trading with them on the previous days. The aborigines had not wanted them to go, and by gestures had tried to entice them to stay, indicating the dangers of falling into the hands of another tribe, who would spear them and even, so their expressive miming seemed to indicate, eat them. Finding their overtures rejected, the aborigines became petulant and Captain Fraser had a threatening spear thrust in his face that grazed his cheek and drew blood. The warning was taken, and like Baxter, Captain Fraser had counselled his party to passive obedience. True to form, the aborigines had taken advantage of this lack of resistance by removing all their clothes with the exception of Mrs Fraser's sou'wester which seemed once again, apparently on account of its tarry smell, to have some sort of quality of taboo. The marauders had then retired with their booty and left the fugitives to continue on their way.

Happy to be re-united, they decided at all costs to stay together, and for several days moved slowly along the beach, travelling mainly at night while the aborigines were asleep, the only landmarks the craggy outline of Indian Head and the whitened vertebrae and ribs of a clean-picked whale. One afternoon, sheltering under scrub-oak from the torrid sun, they heard chattering voices in the undergrowth and before they could rise to their feet were surrounded by a band of painted warriors who shook their spears

45

ferociously and showed none of the initial reserve of earlier encounters. Their copper colouring, produced by rubbing themselves in dust from the red rocks that marked the beginning of their territory, indicated that they belonged to another and apparently more warlike group.

Captain Fraser, by now resigned to his fate and mustering what dignity he could command in his naked state, made signs to the apparent leader of the aggressive party, an old man with an unusually long beard, that he wished to parley rather than defend himself. The grotesque elder, who was presumably a sort of witch doctor, approached with an air of immense self-importance, laid hold of Captain Fraser's chin, and rubbed his hands up and down his naked body as if first establishing tangibility, and then his qualities as a work-horse or even, Captain Fraser would probably have felt, as a future meal. Finally, he looked the captain in the eye with a penetrating scrutiny, uttered a violent scream which made the rocks echo, and made a joyful gesticulation to the others who were standing around with looks of urgent anticipation. After the old man had completed his inspection, a member of another tribe came forward and subjected Mrs Fraser, Brown, Baxter and Corralis to the same treatment. Corralis, apparently on account of his dark colour, seemed to excite more appreciation than the others and was immediately led to one side. The scrutineers then withdrew into a huddle and appeared to be discussing the matter. Probably they were arguing the ancestry of their prisoners, for it was their belief that white men were the ghosts of their dead relations returning to visit them from the Land of Spirits, a theory based on the fact that in ritual cremations, or in preparation for a meal of human flesh, they had noticed that after their dusky bodies had been scorched and flayed, the underskin was invariably white (Appendix IV).

However, no one seemed to claim them as kinsmen, but rather as possible slaves, for shortly afterwards various savages of the two colourations—copper and black—came forward and each grabbing a victim, bundled them unceremoniously into the woods.

Mrs Fraser, to her chagrin and distress, was ignored as apparently of no interest or value, and left entirely to herself. Her pathetic attempts to follow were frustrated by the mock passing of spears and ferocious face-makings of the rearguard.

V

The Domestication Of Mrs Fraser

Mrs Fraser made no further attempt to follow her husband. She felt she had seen him for the last time and was doomed to remain forever naked, unwanted and alone. But after a meal of shellfish from the rocks her resilience returned and she began to elaborate ideas of self-preservation and escape.

A high-pitched chattering disturbed her reverie and she turned to see a group of female aborigines approaching down the bluff. All, from nubile girls to ancient crones, seemed to her of repellent ugliness. They stopped short and stood looking at her as if she was an unfamiliar animal; then, pointing at her derisively, they began to laugh and giggle. As if to shield herself from their malicious gaze, Mrs Fraser's arms went instinctively to her swollen breasts. This modest gesture seemed to aggravate them, for, yelling shrilly, some picked up handfuls of wet sand and threw it at her naked body, so that she became, in her own words, "stuccoed all over". The effect of the salty sand on her newly sunburned skin was excruciatingly painful. Her tormentors next submitted her to a close and almost clinical examination, demonstrating physical differences, prodding, pinching and pulling her hair.

Had she talked the language, Mrs Fraser might have been able to dominate the situation, but the total incomprehensibility of their rapid chatter must have given her a feeling of desperate insufficiency. She put up no resistance as they grabbed her arms and held her tight. Now a prisoner of the female element of the tribe, she was jostled along by her excited captors to their camp in the woods at a speed which made it difficult for her to maintain that dignified progress she felt the situation demanded; the prouder her posture the more they seemed to be trying to humiliate her, slapping her with sticks and mimicking her walk with wicked parody.

Their sleazy encampment, disposed round a shallow pond at the bottom of a hollow, was a haphazard collection of crude shelters—mere strips of bark and wattle laid over hoops of withy. *Dilly-bags*, their simple grass-woven hold-alls, hung from the branches of trees, smoky fires burned, families squatted around, lean and mangy curs rummaged among old bones and garbage. Tribesmen, bedizened with paint, tinkered with their weapons and hardly looked up as the female prisoner passed. Pot-bellied children ran up and stared, a yellow dog snarled and nipped her ankles. She searched urgently around her for a glimpse of her husband or the others, but was unable to catch sight of them.

On the edge of the camp, a woman was sitting near a fire with a baby on her back and another child crying by the embers. She was covered all over her breasts and down one side of her body with ulcerated yaws. An aged granny, toothless and hairless, picked up the baby and thrust it into Mrs Fraser's arms; pointing to the mother's sores and to her own desiccated chest, she indicated that the child was in need of feeding by another. The granny then started kneading Mrs Fraser's heavy breasts and there were sighs of knowing appreciation from the surrounding onlookers as she held the baby's head downwards and it began to suck. Mrs Fraser felt only horror at this action for, according to her description, it was "one of the most deformed and ugly-looking brats my eyes ever beheld". This pathetic specimen, it seemed, was to be her special charge and she accepted it in as charitable a spirit as she could muster, carrying it around in their fashion on her shoulders with its legs around her neck. Its age and sex are not known; aboriginal women often breast-fed their children to the age of four.

Had she arrived amongst the aborigines under different circumstances, as a missionary or a civilised lady visiting simple savages,

Mrs Fraser would no doubt have been quite in her element and given selfless service to those less fortunate than she. The ladies of the tribe could have been taught needlework and hygiene and methods of cookery other than their endless broiling. Instruction in the English language might have followed and a Sunday School to teach simple scripture been established. But in her present position her status as a superior being did not seem to be in any way appreciated. Even a dog, to which she had given an understanding pat, had bitten her sharply in the hand. The baby's mother did, however, seem grateful, for she threw her food from time to time, but likely as not children or dogs would pounce on it first and all she got were scraps and bones. The aged grandmother was continually complaining and pulled Mrs Fraser's hair as soon as the brat began to cry.

In the heat of the day the unfortunate mother would make her new slave cover her with leaves. Mrs Fraser thought this was to keep off the flies which swarmed around the camp and literally feasted off the open sores, but it was more likely to be a primitive cure based on healing moulds in the decaying vegetation. This daily leaf-covering reminded her of the story of the Babes in the Wood, who were thus covered by robin redbreasts, and she whimsically, and possibly in the manner in which a nurse patronises a difficult patient, used to address the sick woman as "Robina".

Aboriginal babies are born light-skinned and, instead of washing them, one of the first things their mothers did was to darken them with grease and soot mixed with their own milk. As if offended by her whiteness and perhaps wishing to put her in the "uniform" of a domestic, or more probably to protect her from sunburn and insect bites, a group of older women took Mrs Fraser aside and, laying her down on the forest floor, rubbed her all over with an evil-smelling mixture of charcoal and lizard grease, so that after a few applications her skin became almost as dark as theirs. They painted her with stripes and circles peculiar to their community, mixing their powdered colour with spittle; they put gums in her hair which they adorned with the bright feathers of parakeet and cockatoo.

It may be wondered what the aborigines thought of the unattractive and possibly malevolent spirits who had come amongst them. They were extra mouths to feed at a time when food was very scarce. Mrs Fraser had to work like any other woman even if she was a "ghost". Her domestication was difficult. They made her go out into the woods to collect sticks and laughed at her when she bent over to pick them up with her hands rather than with her feet, or failed to balance them on her head like everyone else. They tried to make her climb trees as they did, cutting notches in the bark and using a liana as a loop around the trunk. When she could not master the art, at which even small children were expert, they would put fire-sticks to her lacerated legs and bottom. She was made to search out wild bees' nests in hollow trees, rarely receiving more than the acidy grubs or empty comb for her labours. Happily the bees were stingless and smaller than a fly. Should she fail to return with a nest they would make her breathe in their faces on suspicion of secret gorging in the foliage, a lack of generosity that may have been aggravated by her shocked refusal to eat the honey as they did—dipping in a spongy finger made from tree bark and passing it round to be sucked by each in turn.

While they ate goodies like snake, lizard, or the fat and nutty beetle grub they called *buruga** that nestled in rotten logs, she had only pounded fern root (*bungwall*), entrails, an occasional fish-head, and white ant larvae reserved for the women and very old men. Once they threw her a tuber of caladium, and laughed when she chewed the fiercely peppery root they used to cook. Her mouth was so badly burned that she could not eat for days.

Except for the hunting of game, it was the women's duty to

* The east coast natives used to pile logs of wood in the mangrove swamps to be infested by the grubs of the cobra moth, which they then harvested. The *buruga* or *witchetty* grub, about five inches long, was the larva of a longicorn beetle. It is eaten raw or roasted, and has been described as having "the consistency of rice-pudding".

do all the work for the men, who treated them with scant consideration. The most menial tasks were reserved for Mrs Fraser —fetching water in the earliest hours of the morning, watching babies, pounding grass-seed with a crude pestle and mortar, and putting wood on the fires throughout the night. She was given a "digging stick" to probe for roots and yams, a crude wooden instrument pointed at one end which the women often used in blow-for-blow combat with each other and sometimes on her as chastisement for her shortcomings. They made her dive for lily bulbs in the ponds or *billabongs*, mocking her ungainly efforts to locate them underwater. The children of the camp, whose friendship she tried to win, spied on her, grabbed her scraps of food, and practised throwing their sticks and toy boomerangs at her as she went about her work.

Mrs Fraser viewed the squalor that surrounded her with distaste and disdain and seems to have treated the aborigines as patronisingly as if they had been impoverished tinkers on an Orkney hill. She loftily described how the women never washed and how dirt and ashes adhered to their sooty bodies, and how they used to pick the unusually large brown lice from each other's hair and eat them in the manner of monkeys. Her superior attitude and attempts at improving their manners may have angered the touchy natives and inspired them to further chicanery. They practised depilation on themselves, and Mrs Fraser's body hairs had been plucked more painfully than was necessary. Like her mistress she herself was in no great physical shape—as well as being burned by fire-sticks and beaten with *waddys*, her body was bitten by horse-flies, sandflies and mosquitoes and covered with irritating sores. The poor woman cannot have had a moment's pleasure in her day.

Snakes became a familiar feature in her life, from the poisonous species which the natives avoided, to fourteen-foot constrictors, torpid in the winter chill, which dozed among the wreaths of ferns that clustered round the tree-tops. The python-like carpet snake was a great delicacy to be cooked with special care, baked with aromatic leaves in an oven made of stones. Though she rarely received a share, Mrs Fraser observed its preparation and disposal with interest—the choicest portion, the fat, was handed round to greedy mouths in long strings; heart, liver and lungs were allocated to favoured diners, and then the white flesh was distributed. Nothing was wasted, even the backbone was crushed between stones and sucked and chewed with relish.

In the fifth week of her enslavement Mrs Fraser came upon her husband in a forest clearing. He was bent double, desperately trying to drag a heavy log through the tangled undergrowth. She did not describe the effect on her feelings of the encounter, but later reported the outline of their conversation and its dramatic conclusion. To her first reproachful question: "Why did you leave me on the beach?" Captain Fraser replied that he had expected her to follow. Shortly after their separation, he told her, his group had been joined by other members of the long-boat party, including Darge and Youlden, who had also been captured. They had now been apportioned to neighbouring tribes, but he and Brown were living nearby with a family group of Mrs Fraser's own tribe. He told her how he had been treated as a slave and beaten if he did not work hard enough, a frequent occurrence owing to his sickness and starvation. He did not think he could continue to work much longer and, according to her account, said imploringly: "Eliza, wilt thou help me with this tree?" Hearing his pathetic reason—"Because thou art now stronger than me!"—Mrs Fraser proposed returning to help him after she had disposed of her own load. A group of natives suddenly appeared in the distance and she suggested withdrawing into the bush. His unexpectedly placid response: "My dear, they will not meddle with me!" was soon to be brutally contradicted. At the aborigines' approach Mrs Fraser had hidden behind a large tree and watched the whole scene from cover. The men, it appeared, had just returned from an unsuccessful hunting expedition and being hungry were more than usually out of temper. They began to scream at Captain Fraser and to poke him with their clubs and spears. The enfeebled man tried to drag his log according to their directions, but was unable to stand and kept falling to the ground. In a gust of capricious petulance one of the hunters thrust his spear at Captain Fraser's back, and his wife was horrified to see it emerge several inches through his chest.* She ran forward and pulled the weapon from his body and then seems to have fainted. In reply to a question put to her later, she stated with unusual charity: "I do not think it was their intention to kill my husband. I believe the man who cast the spear intended only to wound him, but it went in at his shoulders. I saw no blood, and I pulled the spear from his body. He turned his face to me and said, 'Eliza, I am gone for ever!' and from his mouth an immense quantity of blood spouted, and he at once died. When I recovered from my insensibility I could see no trace of the body and I never could learn anything about it afterwards; but it was better that I did not, for I have seen them dispose of their bodies, and it is dreadful beyond anything in the world."

The unfortunate Brown was the next to die and his preliminary agony was witnessed by Baxter, who described it in a subsequent statement:—

"We were now only six in number and all separated with different tribes. Mr Brown was the next sufferer. In the morning previous he was again brought to the tribe I was stopping with, and they were more than usually kind to him, which he remarked to me. They, having caught some fish this morning, offered him part of one, but as we had to go and fetch the wood and water for them, he said they would let it remain till he returned. I now

---

* The aborigines of Fraser Island are said to have been exceptionally cruel. In 1857 the *Seabelle* was wrecked off Breaksea Spit, at the north end. Two years later, having heard reports of survivors, Captain Amard made a search in the *Coquette* from Maryborough. He found two young white girls living with the natives in the area where the *Stirling Castle* party landed. The elder, Kitty, who was seventeen, said that all the crew had been murdered. Presumably to accord with their captors' ideals of beauty, the girls had been disfigured—their noses flattened and their mouths cut about. They were placed in an institution in Sydney.

desired him to eat it first before he went, seeing they were displeased at his putting it away; but however he would not eat it then. Having finished mine, we set off for the wood; and after we had returned, we found two of the red tribe with the tribe we were staying with. This being unusual, I knew not what to think; but, however, they took the deceased by the hand and made signs to him to go with them for something to eat. Upon my offering to go with them, they made me return back; and about two hours afterwards they came and took me in the same way, and by the same signs, and after going about a mile, I was horror-struck to find him tied to a tree, hand and foot, and a slow fire made at his feet, but much more to see one of the men on a stake close by, and writhing in the greatest agony, their last words being to let their mothers know of their untimely end."

The other man was Michael Denny, who emerges from the story for the first and last time on this unfortunate occasion.

But it seems that the unhappy Brown did not meet death by burning at the stake after all, and that his exhibition to Baxter was in the nature of a warning what to expect if he did not work hard enough. In fact Brown, badly burned about the legs and back, attempted to make his way to a water-hole. Nobody would help him. The tribe had rejected him. Like Philoctetes, he was left alone to die with his stinking wounds. As Mrs Fraser described it: "He was so bad that the tribe would not let him stay close. He lay on the opposite bank of the water-hole, under a powerful sun, and hot wind. He called to me to come and kill him. He raved all day. I endeavoured often to carry him water in my hat, but was always beaten. I got close to Mr Brown. Life was extinct, he was covered with red ants. For this last look at my poor friend I was dreadfully beaten."

VI

The Hunger Of John Baxter

The crew of the long-boat were now reduced and dispersed. Captain Fraser, Brown and Denny were dead, Mrs Fraser, Youlden, Darge and Corralis, Dayman and the boy Carey had been moved by canoe to the mainland. Baxter, Doyle, and Elliot were on different parts of the island. Baxter had tried hard to get himself taken to the mainland with the others, who had been making plans to escape. But the aborigines seemed aware of what was in his mind: as if to gratify his desires they once paddled him out from the shore towards the opposite side; after a short distance they bundled him into the water and made him swim back again, taking a childish delight in their unpleasant deception.

Doyle and Elliot, desperate to escape, had the idea of swimming the channel, which at its narrowest point was about three miles wide and with a strong current. Baxter tried to dissuade them, but one day, impelled by their frustrations, they rushed compulsively into the water and struck out for the opposite shore. The aborigines did not attempt to pursue them or hurl their spears. They stood watching until, almost as if they had been expecting it, the dorsal fin of some local shark cleaved up, and they laughed and *coo-eed* as the sailors disappeared beneath the disturbed and bloodied water.

Baxter's tribe, members of the Kabi group, were basically a shore people, living mainly on fish and molluscs and making only occasional expeditions into the interior in search of meat. Bream, mullet and ray were their main catch and they would spear them in the shallows with great accuracy or drive them into a net, cunningly made from wood fibre, fixed to a wooden bow. Baxter had the job of beating the water to drive the shoals into the net, a task in which he was sometimes aided by the species of dolphin that cruised offshore and, almost in collusion with the fishermen, seemed to herd the fish towards them. The arrival of these co-operative mammals was greeted with cries of joy and they were treated with the familiarity of old friends and rewarded with part of the catch for their assistance.

Sometimes a stranded whale would feed the tribe for a week. Once he heard urgent cries of "Yuangan! Yuangan!" and joined excited tribesmen as they caught a massive weed-eating sea-cow, or dugong (Appendix V) in the wide-meshed nets specially made for the purpose. The wretched mammal, wheezing and gasping in the shallows, was speared to death by forty impassioned hunters and dragged on to the beach in triumph, half a ton of greatly needed protein. Tribes from miles around gathered to eat this famous delicacy, and they gorged on the carcase for a day until nothing but a skeleton remained.

Poor Baxter got none. He was cast as a slave and like a slave he was the last to feed, which at a season when all were hungry meant he was virtually starved. Even if the catch was good he seldom got more than a fish-head to eat, though he fared better with the *bungwall* prepared by the women and brought down to the beach to trade with their menfolk for a share in the catch. They called him "Curri", which meant "hungry" in the local dialect. It was a word he had picked up from the children and had frequent occasion, like them, to use. His cries of "*curri!*", as his captors wolfed their meal, can have brought little more response than the mocking repetition of his pathetic plea.

The only occasion he was offered a share in the main course, he did not feel like taking advantage of it. Baxter, who was a simple man and not given to over-statement, described the horrific incident in a subsequent terse report: "The child was a boy about five years old, and he took a piece of fish and one of the men, I believe the father, struck him with a waddie. I afterwards saw the boy dead, and they put part of the flesh to the fire and afterwards ate it. They offered me the heart and part of the liver, and then dragged me about by the hair when I refused."

Food was more plentiful when they took him on a mainland hunt. His role was to carry weapons and help set the nets for kangaroo, emu or wildfowl, which at that time of the year seldom seemed to enmesh any game. Once they speared a wallaby and as the creature was being beaten to death with clubs Baxter noticed a very small baby creeping from its mother's pouch. He picked it up but one of the men tore it from him and threw it onto the embers of the fire. Before it was half roasted he took it out and devoured the hindquarters in a mighty mouthful. The hungry sailor was thrown the rest and ate it gratefully.

When his hunting party was visiting another tribe, Baxter was greeted by a bizarre figure who stood out among his fellows by his height and the length of his beard, moustachios and hair, which was tied up in a huge bunch on the crown of his head. His skin was decorated with white and yellow paint and his chest was deeply scarified in the native manner. Stuck through his nose Baxter thought he recognised the hollow stem of a clay pipe. The extraordinary wild-eyed apparition gabbled at him in a language that contained certain recognisable words—"commandant", "bacca", and "bleedin' lime-kilns". He was an escaped convict from Moreton Bay, at large for so long that he had almost forgotten his native tongue.

Though at first the convict found difficulty in finding words, he was so gratified to meet a fellow white that he chattered on endlessly in complicated English, asking questions about Moreton Bay and the characters he remembered. He had apparently taken off six years ago from the lime-burning station opened by Commandant Logan fifteen miles from the settlement to provide mortar for the building of Brisbane.* When he learned that Baxter

* Captain Logan, the disciplinarian commandant of the Moreton Bay Penal Settlement, had discovered "Limestone Hills", near modern Ipswich, and set up kilns there. A few convicts with a guard of soldiers, burnt 300–400 bushels of lime a week.

was not an escapee like himself, but a shipwrecked seaman, he became more guarded in his conversation, refusing to give his name and extracting a promise to say nothing of their meeting should he ultimately get back to civilisation. This was a sensible reticence as Baxter later indiscreetly announced that the convict had relations in London, had been transported to New South Wales for fourteen years and, having committed some further crime in the colony, been sent to Moreton Bay "for the term of his natural life". This absconder was also met on another occasion by Darge, who revealed in London that his name was Banks and his native nickname "Tallboy".

After months of wandering, said "Tallboy" Banks, he had fallen in with the tribe he was now attached to. He had first been held as a slave, but one of the women had taken a fancy to him and he had gone to live in her shelter and, though unclaimed as an ancestor, had been accepted as a member of the tribe. He pointed at the small brats playing in the dust, who seemed to have only the slightest traces of their father's physical heritage. His jealous wife showed none of the social graces but danced up and down grimacing, angry to be excluded from the conversation or perhaps worried that this visitor from the Land of Spirits might somehow take her husband from her.

Baxter did in fact try to organise an escape, assuring the convict that if he could bring him back to Moreton Bay he would be rewarded with remission. But "Tallboy" seemed content with his limited life and showed no desire to return to "civilisation" even as a free man. Here he had status and could measure himself against men in their own skills. Lack of food was a problem, but soon, he said, they would be going up into the mountains in search of honey. According to Baxter he said exultantly: "We shall get fat when we get up yonder!" And an even better event to look forward to, it seemed, was the great feast on the *bunya-bunya* pinetrees, at their best every three years, when tribes from far and wide gathered in the forests for weeks at a time to guzzle compulsively on the succulent nuts (Appendix VII). Those were great "*borees*", he explained, when every sort of diversion took place from the discussion of weighty affairs, real and ritual battles, ceremonial dancing, competitions of prowess, the initiation of young men, and dangerous abductions of desirable virgins from the camps of neighbouring tribes.

The hunting was bad. Some possums laboriously smoked from hollow trees, a single wallaby and a desiccated fatless emu had been their only bag. The party soon returned to a diet of fish and fernroot. "Curri"* did all he could to please his captors and so obtain more food. He played with the children, sparred with the young men, and amused the ladies with somersaults and handsprings. To some extent he seems to have endeared himself to them, but his role as slave never changed and starvation always stalked behind him.

---

* It is possible that Baxter's native name was derived from the Kabi word for the grey possum—*Kuru-i*. See Darge's testimony (page 140) for usage of *corru* meaning 'hungry'.

VII

Her Virtue In Jeopardy

Conditions for Mrs Fraser were not improving. She was soon moved to the mainland side of the island protected by Breaksea Spit, where instead of surf and sand there was a soft lap of sheltered tidal water ebbing and flooding through muddy creeks and across vast estuarine flats. Here there was a different sort of food-gathering. She particularly hated being sent into the mangrove swamps to collect mussels and the elusive mud-crabs, big as dinner plates, that scuttled backwards into the sand faster than she could grab them. To find them she had to walk up to her ankles in the spiky ooze among the stunted, root-exposed trees. Nature seemed to conspire against her: leeches attached themselves to her legs, mosquitoes covered her arms like fur, harmless birds like pelicans, egrets and black swans appeared sinister; mud skippers glared with protuberant and apparently malevolent eyes and cohorts of small blue soldier-crabs investigated with interested, but to her unpleasant, purpose. She told people later that she was terrified out of her wits and unless she returned with a full *dilly-bag* she would be driven out again with blows.

Sometimes she would wander in the humid gloom of the rainforest, dwarfed by the overwhelmingly tall and straight satinay trees and palms. Jumping ants stung viciously, big spiders strung their webs face-high across the trails. When she thought she was not being spied on she would sit among the ferns and try to bring her mind back to her real identity, but the chatterings of parakeets, and the strange cracks of the whipbirds and the hectic susurrations of cicadas in the foliage made her feel she was going out of her mind.

The Kabi tribe seemed to have a specific place for slaves in their social system, and though all their women were in a sense slaves, Mrs Fraser was a slave to slaves. The women intensified their cruel treatment, whether through resentment, jealousy or natural predilection. They would not let her sleep in the shelters, nor, doubtless, would she have wished even to enter such insanitary shelters, and although she was allowed to lie near the fire in a hollow scraped in the ground and cover herself with dried ferns and grasses, the winter nights were chilly and damp and she woke every morning shivering and soaked in dew. On a diet of roots and scraps she had become thin and gaunt; the sun had shrivelled her skin and her hair was grotesquely matted. She cannot have looked an object of great beauty, yet to the tribesmen she might have seemed as exotic as a Cleopatra. She was aware that they watched her with interest and that lustful eyes followed her as she walked about the camp; black forms would creep about her at night as she lay naked and alone beneath the Southern Cross. Many young aboriginal men have physiques of considerable beauty and it may be that Mrs Fraser in her turn was interested in them to a degree she would be unlikely to have admitted even to herself.

The Kabi people had two words denoting marriage—*bida-mathi*, which implied agreement by parents or guardian, and *dhommanthi*, or marriage without consent or by capture. There were also, it seems, occasions when a system of *jus primae noctis* was the custom among senior members of the tribe. *Corroborees* were great occasions for the allocation and abduction of women; sometimes a female would be set apart in an isolated position, inviting capture; should she prove a disappointment to her captor she would be turned over to his group as common property. At the death of her husband a widow belonged to his brother or nearest male relative, who might give her away if he did not fancy her. Mrs Fraser, now with no claimant to her person, was inevitably sought after by unsatisfied men in a society that laid down strict and complicated rules of intermarriage within the same family groups. It is clear that she had some unpleasant experiences, but her inconsistency and natural reticence in recounting them has led to a lack of credible information on the subject. Her most reliable biographer, John Curtis,* writing for a prudish public, is aggravatingly unspecific about her sexual adventures, confining himself to such unsubstantiated statements as: "We have in our possession facts connected with the brutal treatment of this helpless woman, which, if we dared to publish them, would excite a voluntary shudder of horror and disgust in every well-regulated mind."

Mrs Fraser was suddenly moved southwards with the tribe. Carrying more than her share of the camp chattels she was hurried through the scrubby terrain, the women barely finding time to gather food on the way as was their usual duty. They were making for the important *corroboree* grounds, forty miles to the south, beside Lake Cootharaba, the big inland water fed by the meandering Noosa river. Here, among strange domed hills, tribes from far and wide had assembled to perform in the huge sandy ring complicated ceremonies of initiation,† mock warfare, dancing and general get-together.

Mrs Fraser was a prime exhibit at the gathering and it was to inspect her, the first white woman they had ever seen, that they had been called together. She was placed on a crude stage at the top of the ceremonial path leading to the ring, and around her the painted savages of her tribe proudly sang and mimed, to the rhythmic beat of percussion sticks, the latest drama—the arrival of "ghosts" from the sea, the spearing of the captain, the drowning

* "Shipwreck of the *Stirling Castle*, etc." by John Curtis, George Virtue, London, 1837.

† As well as circumcision, some aboriginal tribes in Australia practised sub-incision, or perforation of the urethra. Young men were submitted to this excruciating ordeal as a test of manhood. The youth was held down over the backs of crouching colleagues, while the "surgeon" performed his crude operation with shell or flint. Sub-incision suggests an elementary form of contraception, but this is not thought to have been the intention. Organs which had been treated in this manner were referred to by the settlers as "whistle-cocks".

of the sailors, the domestication of the she-ghost, and other significant events.

On such an occasion, where women were traditionally exposed to adventure and possible abduction, Mrs Fraser may well have had the sort of experience Curtis refers to. It was presumably at the *corroboree* ground that she claimed to have undergone the unpleasant adventure that questionably just stopped short of a "fate worse than death". The story is told in a small book published under her name in 1837 in America by Charles Webb of New York. Despite such Red Indian terminology as "papoose", "tomahawk", "wigwam", and "squaw", for the benefit of American readers, and some obvious invention in dialogue, the book, entitled "Narrative of the Capture, Sufferings, and Miraculous Escape of Mrs Eliza Fraser", bears something of the stamp of her personality. The following extract purports to describe how she formed an attachment for her mistress's brother-in-law. The story of the championing of the captain's lady by a savage nobler than the rest may have covered a more romantic relationship than she was prepared to admit:

"Although I had now been more than six weeks in the power of the savages, and in that time suffered much, not only by being compelled to perform tasks that my strength would hardly admit of but by reason of being exposed to the scorching rays of the sun by day, and the damp air at night, and with an allowance of food (if food it can be called) hardly sufficient to satisfy the calls of nature, yet, during the whole period independent of the hard labour and privations to which they had subjected me I had neither experience from or discovered any disposition on the part of the savages to subject my person to brutal insult; until a few days after the death of my husband, when, the reader may imagine how great must have been my surprise, as well as disgust, to be visited by one of the most ugly and frightful-looking Indians that my eyes ever beheld or that the whole island probably contained, with proposals that, "as I had lost my mate, I should become his squaw!" Having made every sign possible significant of the detestation and abhorrence in which he was held by me, and that death by his hands would be far preferable to my becoming his companion or 'squaw', as he was pleased to term me, I endeavoured to represent to him my willingness to become his slave, and to obey him in all his reasonable commands—but, this would not suffice. I must (he represented to me) either voluntarily become his 'mate' or become so by compulsion! that he was a chief, and that my late master and mistress had relinquished to him all claim to me; and, that but a short time would be allowed to me to consider of it, and to decide! I was now indeed placed in a situation more horrid than I had ever any previous conception of! yea, even so much as to be compelled to decide, and that too, immediately, whether to become the willing companion and associate of a wild barbarous savage, or voluntarily suffer myself to become the defenceless victim of brutal outrage! In this dreadful dilemma, kind providence once more directed me to apply to and plead for the interposition of my late mistress's brother, entreating him that if he should not succeed in defeating the designs of the old chief, who was apparently between sixty and seventy years of age, to do me the kindness either to stab me in the heart, or to knock me on the head with his tomahawk, as death, even in that savage manner, would be preferable to that of yielding to the desires of him who professed to have power to do as he pleased with me!

"Soon I had the satisfaction to see that my application for relief was not made in vain; and soon after, to my sorrow, that I had but very little more cause to rejoice than to mourn, as by his kind act of interference my benefactor lost his life! The savage chief finding himself opposed in his designs by one of inferior rank, a challenge ensued, which being accepted by him by whom I had been uniformly treated with much humanity. They met and fought with their knives, but the contest with such weapons, was as short as it was fatal. My friend received a wound from his antagonist, which reaching the heart, produced almost instantaneous death! and accompanying his last dying groan might be heard the hideous and exulting whoop of the savage monster by whose hands he fell, who now finding all obstacles removed and no one who dared oppose him, without further ceremony or dealing, seized me by the shoulder, and fiend-like forced me within the enclosure of his dismal and filthy cabin, but before he had time to accomplish his designs the God of mercy interposed, and sent one, as if commissioned expressly for the purpose, from Heaven, to rescue me, not from the devouring jaws of a ravenous lion, but from the hands of a savage ruffian, far more to be dreaded!" . . .

VIII

The Irish Convict

Leaving Baxter slowly starving on Great Sandy Island and Mrs Fraser in an embarrassing predicament on the mainland, let us approach the story from another direction. On Monday 8th August Lieutenant Charles Otter of the 4th (Kings Own) Regiment had obtained a week's leave and sailed out with a few friends and a convict crew into Moreton Bay. No doubt he found it a relief to get away from the oppressive atmosphere and limited society of the penal settlement, where his unit was charged with the security of the colony and the guarding of the prisoners (Appendix VII). Having called in at the Pilot Station near the treacherous sandbanks at the mouth of the bay, the party landed on Bribie Island to catch turtle and shoot wildfowl.

While banging off at the innumerable duck, Otter suddenly saw three "blacks" emerging from the bush and raised his gun to cover them. He was amazed to hear one of them call, "Don't shoot, sir! We're British subjects! Shipwrecked sailors!"* The group in fact consisted of Darge and Corralis, last seen carried away to the mainland in captivity, and an aborigine guide to whom they had promised the standard reward of *gilla-gilla* (fish-hooks) and a *moco* (hatchet) to conduct them through the complicated topography of forest and swamp to Moreton Bay. Why he had led them across the channel, named Pumice Stone Passage by Flinders, on to Bribie Island is not clear, for had they

* This recalls the story of James Morrill, sole survivor of the barque *Peruvian*, lost in 1846, who spent 17 years with the tribes of North Queensland. Such was his confusion at being confronted by a white shepherd with a gun that he shouted, "Don't shoot, I'm a British *object*!"

not met Otter they might well have remained there a very long time before anyone else visited the place.

Darge blurted out that there was a third member of their party who, too weak to keep up with them, had been abandoned in the bush twenty five miles back. A couple of Otter's convict crew, aided by the aborigine guide, were sent back to look for him and finally returned to the rendezvous carrying a pathetic specimen on their shoulders. It was Harry Youlden, who was amazed to see his comrades again and weakly swore he thought he'd been a "gonner". Otter's augmented party then returned to the settlement as quickly as they could.

By a strange coincidence a story of survivors from the *Stirling Castle* had just reached Moreton Bay from another source, retailed by a small group of natives from the north. They had hiked several hundred miles to visit their friend the convict John Graham, who as a "constable" had a certain freedom of movement around the settlement. Graham, known to them as "Moilow", had lived among their people for seven years as the "ghost" of a departed tribesman. Members of this tribe had paid him regular visits in the past, but this time they brought with them some young men from an area farther to the north. These strangers had some special news—the arrival among them of other "ghosts", including a "she-ghost"! Documentary evidence enables us to follow in some detail the story of how a convict came to be the recipient of such interesting information.

Graham was an Irishman from Dundalk, Co. Louth, a little fellow only five feet tall, a simple labourer who at the age of 24 had stolen 6¾ pounds of hemp and been sentenced to seven years' transportation. After a spell on the prison hulk moored in Cork harbour he had been shipped to Sydney on the *Hooghley* along with a hundred and ninety-five other felons.

On arrival in Australia, transportees were generally "assigned" to free settlers, who had found in the availability of such cheap labour an added inducement to immigration. Physical conditions were no worse and probably better than many of them had known in rural Britain; liberal rations and accommodation were provided and a small wage paid for work done; additional money could be made doing odd jobs in their spare time and there were opportunities to congregate for a drink or a game of cards at one of the numerous shebeens. Indeed conditions were so reasonable that the authorities at home tried to counteract this impression by publicising deterrent aspects (Appendix IX). But assigned convicts were at the mercy of their employers, who were in a powerful position to exploit them and were apt to denounce them to the authorities for the smallest insubordination or dereliction from duty. The magistrates were on the side of the masters, and a case brought to Court most likely meant the "cat" or rigorous imprisonment at a penal settlement.* Graham had been "assigned" to John Raine, an ambitious businessman who owned a tidal water mill at Parramatta, then a rural settlement 14 miles north-west of Sydney and site of the "Female Factory", where derelict women, waiting to be hired as servants, wove coarse-cloth used for blankets and the prisoners' clothes.†

Like many other employers of convict labour, Raine had trouble with his staff, and the records show that he several times had them

* To quote Sir George Arthur, then Governor of Van Diemen's Land: "Idleness and insolence of expression, or of looks, anything betraying an insurgent spirit, subject him to the chain-gang or the triangle". In 1836 there were 22,000 summary convictions in New South Wales out of a total convict population of 27,000. In that year 3,000 convicts were flogged or around 108,000 lashes inflicted with the cat-o-nine-tails, mostly for such petty offenses. It should not be thought, however, that all convicts were innocent misused men. There were some deep-dyed rogues among them, and many were guilty of major crimes. Even Foster-Fyans, appointed commandant of Moreton Bay in 1835, and of a benevolent and paternalistic disposition toward his charges, was able to make exceptions, referring to the worst of them as "beyond anything I found in the shape of a human being".

† A contemporary observer, James Bonwick, described the Female Factory at Parramatta, designed to house three hundred women, as "the seat of idleness, the resort of the vicious; the atmosphere was polluted by the fumes of tobacco smoked by the women, and the walls echoed with the shrieks of passion, the peals of foolish laughter, and oaths of common converse. The beginners in the walks of vice associated with the abandoned veterans of crime."

up before the magistrates. Graham was probably among the "eight men returned to Government" referred to in his deposition of 15th August 1826 laid against the proprietor of a "sly", or unlicensed, grog-shop:—

"John Raine Esq., deposed that his servants have, for a considerable time past, been in the habit of becoming intoxicated; that his mill is in the habit of being robbed by his servants, and their clothing, bedding, etc. are sold; that, in consequence of the insubordinate state they had arrived at, he was compelled to return eight men to Government a few days ago, to his serious detriment; that he, in consequence, made every enquiry, and exerted himself to ascertain where they had been harboured; that on Sunday morning he sent his servant with a letter to the coach, and to obtain some of the necessaries for dinner; that he returned home about nine o'clock, intoxicated; that deponent enquired of him where he had got his spirits, promising to look over his error if he told him; that he told the deponent that he had obtained the liquor at Kerton's and had paid for the same; that he absented himself yesterday again, without liberty; that deponent did personally detect him in the house of Mary Kane, or Kennedy, tippling and drinking spirits, which he (the deponent) had tasted; that the said Mary Kane he had also summoned, to answer for harbouring three of his servants tippling on the preceeding evening, and that he was prepared to produce evidence to that effect. He further stated, on oath, he had reason to believe that his servants had become more insubordinate and were continually intoxicated, and consequently their harbourers had evidently become more open in their transactions . . ."

The specific charge against Graham was petty larceny, a repetition of his original offense, and for this and possibly some other minor blots on his record such as described in Raine's deposition, he was sentenced, on 11th October 1826, to seven years' penal servitude at Moreton Bay, where the disciplinary excesses of Commandant Logan had reached the ears of every man in Sydney. Three days after Christmas he was shipped off by sea under military guard. With forty convicts battened down in the hold, chained by their ankles to the deck, it was six days before the schooner reached the penal colony two hundred miles to the north.

Founded the previous year, the prison settlement at Moreton Bay was then uncomfortably sited near the mouth of the river, before removing upstream to what is now Brisbane. In comparison with life at Parramatta it was by intention something of a hell camp. Cut off from outside contacts, convicts were crowded in rough barracks, supervised by corrupt and brutal overseers, and if sentenced to the "iron gang", put to work for long hours in leg-chains on such back-breaking tasks as road building, tree felling, lime-burning, and land clearance. Punishment was frequent and, during Commandant Logan's* regime, extreme. Some men had received hundreds of lashes, strapped to the triangle and whipped with the cat until the flesh hung in shreds from their backs, or, if the scourger was an artist at his job, until the skin was pulpy with blood but unbroken. There were several cases of desperate men murdering their companions with a view to achieving on the gallows an earlier end to an intolerable life.

To escape "Logan of the Lash" an unusual number of convicts took to the woods, but few got far, reduced to starvation by inexperience or brought in by aborigines for the standard reward of a hatchet or fish-hooks. Graham was more fortunate: on July 14th 1827, he broke away from a working-party and managed to cross the open scrubland to gain the thickly forested area that pursuers rarely penetrated. Always a country boy, he had studied

* Patrick Logan was born in Ireland in 1792. He served with his regiment in the Peninsular War and in Canada. Appointed Commandant at Moreton Bay in 1826, he was said to be a just man, though his administration was noted for its harsh discipline and excessive punishment. A keen explorer in his spare time, he was killed on an expedition into the interior in October 1830. He had been attacked by natives, but there were rumours that bushrangers had organized the murder in revenge for his brutal treatment. The ballad A CONVICT'S LAMENT ON THE DEATH OF CAPTAIN LOGAN (published in the Sydney Gazette of 25th November 1830) might well have been sung by Graham and his friends. (Appendix VIII.)

the local aborigines around Parramatta and had learned some of their techniques of survival—ways of finding water, the roots and berries that were edible and methods of catching possums, bandicoots and other small game. After months of wandering in the deepest recesses of the sub-tropical rain forests, keeping out of the way of natives, and fancifully expecting to reach the north coast and find a boat that would take him to China, he blundered into a well-concealed encampment.

Graham knew all about the belief among the aborigines that when their people died they became "ghosts", appropriately white—"When blackfellow die, him jump up white man" was a phrase known to the convicts, who have been credited with its invention. Should the "ghost" be thought to be a relation of an unknown tribe, as seems to have happened in the case of the *Stirling Castle* party, the chances were that he would be rejected and probably put to death, but if recognised as "belonging" to one of their own people, he would be welcomed into the tribe in the name of a departed. Graham was lucky: a not very beautiful widow named "Mamba", probably grasping her only chance of acquiring another mate, claimed him as her dead husband "Moilow" and Graham did not attempt to disillusion her. Perhaps by her prompting, her two sons, "Murrow-Dooling" and "Caravanty", were prepared to recognise him as their father. He also acquired a father-in-law called "Mootemu" and a cousin in almost everyone else in the tribe.

Graham was now one of the family. As "Moilow" he was given his namesake's piece of land called "Thaying" and soon became a trusted and respected member of the small community. Later that year his wife "Mamba" died and he did not feel inclined to take another. After living with her people for six years, learning their language, (which when he joined them, they tactfully assumed he had "forgotten"), taking part in their councils, rituals, hunts and wars, he had suddenly forsaken them, returned to Moreton Bay and surrendered himself to the authorities.

72

There was a reason—all this time in the bush Graham had been conscientiously counting the days; he had worked out that his seven-year sentence was due to expire on October 28th 1833. Three days later he had confidently given himself up at Moreton Bay and claimed to be "time-expired" and therefore due for official "release". But his calculations had not taken into account a Council Instruction of 1830 laying down that time lost by absconding might be made up on recapture "at the discretion of the authorities". The authorities, represented by Captain Clunie, Logan's successor, were inclined to be lenient, and to take into consideration that Graham had brought back valuable information about areas as yet unexplored. There was land out there suitable for future settling; he gave them geographical facts and they were grateful. On November 16th he was told he had to serve another $3\frac{1}{2}$ years, a halving of his original sentence. Good conduct had gained him the position of "constable"* in charge of other prisoners, and his experience in the bush had made him something of a character with officers and convicts alike.

Captain Foster Fyans,† recently appointed commandant of the penal settlement, heard with initial scepticism Graham's version of the tale of survivors told by the aborigines. He was an Irishman himself and wary of the ingratiating ways of some of his charges. In his "Reminiscences", roughed out twenty years later, he sketched his impressions of the visit in his odd staccato style, here punctuated for readability.

* Constables were paid 1s. to 2s. 6d a day according to length of service, as opposed to the 1d. to 2¼d. of the ordinary convict. They did not have to have their hair cut short and could grow whiskers.

† Foster Fyans (1790–1870), an Irishman born in England, served in the Peninsular War and in 1833 came to Sydney to join his regiment the 4th (Kings Own). Soon after his arrival he was sent to the penal colony on Norfolk Island where he helped put down a mutiny among the convicts. He became Commandant at Moreton Bay in 1835. In 1837 he was transferred to Geelong and became a police magistrate and "protector of aborigines". He was said to be a "better policeman than protector", and in 1840 was made commandant of "Border Police", a unit made up of refractory soldiers and "ticket of leave" convicts. He settled in Australia when his regiment left, becoming Sheriff of Geelong in 1853.

"A deputation of seven natives came to see Graham who was an old absconder, and he had remained with their tribe for seven years. He returned to the settlement, where he had to make good all the past years of absence.* The Aborigines of the north side of New South Wales† are generally strong and powerful. This party annually came to see Graham appearing to love and esteem him. On parting it was distressing to witness their grief, yelling and tearing their skin. These poor fellows at all times met with a welcome of kindness from us during the few days they remained, protected from our neighbouring natives, who often wished for a taste of their kidney fat. Twice or thrice during my reign these natives paid their visit, leaving us on good terms with a supply of corn and a blanket to each, never failing to take a store of broken glass for their spears, an article much prized by them. Not many days elapsed after their departure, the deputation again appeared, augmented to twelve. Graham sent for me, informing me that five natives came from the north with the information that a ship had been wrecked, that five men were on shore and a white *lubra*.‡ I almost doubted the sincerity of Graham. I saw the five lads, fine athletic youths, the eldest I suppose not more than sixteen years of age. Not a word could I understand, neither could any of our native boys—Graham was quite conversant, and the only man on the settlement who could interpret for me. Still I had a strong feeling, wishing for another to satisfy myself and save time. Graham accompanied me with the boys to the office— I had one in. Graham put my questions, the answers taken down, and went through until I had examined the five. Their testimony tallied. Graham informed me that he perfectly understood from these boys where the unfortunate people were. Taking a sheet of paper he drew on it the line of the sea coast, with several remarkable objects, placing the native name to each. He then in a rough

* According to the records Graham's remaining time was halved.
† Now Queensland. Queensland was not incorporated as a separate state until 1859.
‡ General settlers' word for an aboriginal woman. Also *gin*.

way introduced equally remarkable objects in the interior, mentioning three lakes, placing the names on every object worthy of notice and as *known* to the tribes in that part of Australia—on this side of this lake the captain died, pointing this out to me, then he asked one of the lads to name the lake where one of the white men was dead. The youth immediately did so—fully corresponding with the name Graham had placed on it. I felt satisfied. I lost all apprehension of Graham's honesty, asking his advice how we should act to preserve the lives of the unfortunate people. This fine fellow replied: 'I shall accompany the blacks and do all I can, but how will it be possible for a female to travel through the bush upwards of four hundred miles?' The difficulty was great, and not to be overcome. Horses were of no use, he stated, in the country where he was to go. I proposed boats. He agreed that the coast was the only way to insure the restoration of the female."

Shortly after the Commandant's urgent discussion, as if to add tangible confirmation to the tribesmen's tale, Lieutenant Otter arrived at the settlement with Darge, Youlden and Corralis. Foster Fyans called them together in his office and investigated their story with particular reference to its geographical locations, calling in Graham to hear the evidence. Darge seemed sly and uncommunicative about the Fraser party, almost as if he wished them well lost. It was the loyal mulatto Corralis who provided the most useful information, and answered Graham's questions with eager concentration.

All agreed that a rescue by sea was the only possible way. Foster Fyans ordered the bell that summoned the convicts from their work to be tolled and gangs came in from all round the perimeter and lined up in the dusty square. When the bedraggled prisoners had been shouted into silence by top-hatted overseers, Fyans explained the situation and called for volunteers, "good rowers", suggesting some sort of reward should the expedition have a successful outcome. Remission was in everybody's mind: at least a hundred men stepped forward, most of whom had never held an oar in their lives. A selection was made and orders were given to Mr Stephen Owen, in charge of the Commissariat, to provision and equip the boats, allowing the convicts the rations of a free sailor but discreetly limiting the issue of rum. Lieutenant Otter, backed by two N.C.O.s of the 4th Regiment, was put in charge of the party, and Graham, the only man who knew the country and people, was appointed interpreter and guide. Captain Foster Fyans exhorted him to do his best and promised him a reward and possible remission should he be instrumental in the safe return of Mrs Fraser.

Thirteen stalwart convict volunteers were selected to row and do the heavy work. Since they played a specific part in the operation, their names and prison particulars are of interest to record:—

Name	Trade	Offence	Sentence
Nathaniel Mitchell	Ploughman	Accessory before the fact of shooting at Mr Thompson	Death, commuted to 7 years.
John Walsh or Cartwright	Mariner	Runaway from Moreton Bay	Remainder of original life
John Williams	Seaman	Receiving Stolen Property	14 years
Christmas Paulgrove	Labourer	Cattle stealing	14 years
Thos. King Thompson	Shoemaker	Burglary	Death, commuted to 14 years
John Phillips	Errand boy	Stealing from a dwelling house	Death, commuted to 14 years
John Shannon	Butcher's boy	Larceny	4 years
John Daley	Weaver	Robbery	7 years
William Brown	Waterman	Assault with intent to murder	2 years
James King	Dyer	Burglary	7 years
Thomas Kinsella	Pedlar	Larceny	7 years
James Pretty	Groom	Highway robbery	7 years

Convict classification also provided as an additional means of identity the name of the ship in which the prisoner arrived in

Australia. Thus, when spoken to, convicts answered to their name and the name of their respective transport, in this case: "Eliza", "Minerva II", "Marquis of Huntley", "Guildford", "Nithsdale", "Victoria", "Champion", "Fairlie", "S. G. Webster", "Waterloo", "Phoenix III", "Cambridge", and "John I". The offenses listed were committed in the Colony. There was one other man, John Lindsay, whose indentures were missing, an occasional lapse on the part of the convict bureaucracy that could lead to a man serving longer than his allotted time while particulars were checked in England, though there had been other occasions when the payment of money had persuaded the convict clerk in charge of records to forge a favourable release date.

On August 11th, three days after Otter's encounter on Bribie Island, the small fleet of whalers set off down river to the sea. In a statement (to the Members of a Select Committee for Transportation, sitting in Victoria in 1857), Foster Fyans, by then retired, proudly described the scene of departure. "The boats were all ready, and on a fine summer's evening there were provisions put into each boat, and fine tarpaulings, and meat hermetically sealed, and everything completely fitted out. I told them when they were going away: 'I send so much spirits with you (a few gallons) and I expect that none will touch those spirits except that the weather is of such a nature as you may require a little, and there is so much wine for this lady.' These boats went away and went down the coast beautifully."

IX

In The Nick Of Time

The rescue party spent the night on Amity Point, the little pilot station on Stradbroke Island that commanded the main channel into Moreton Bay. They set off at dawn next day, and with a strong wind behind them soon reached Caloundra Point at the northern end of Bribie Island. Here they tied up for the night. For all except Graham it was their first taste of an unknown and ominous coast. Next day, Saturday the thirteenth, they sailed on another fifty miles, past the mouth of the Maroochydore, named after the black swans* that thronged its muddy lagoons, and rounding Noosa Head came under its lee into the estuary of the Noosa River, marked on their crude chart as "Huon Mundy's River"† after a famous local warrior.

Graham had planned a rendezvous in this area with one of the natives who had visited him at Moreton Bay, but the only people to be seen on the shore fled into the bush and no contact could be established. Rather than wait, Otter sent Graham off to look for an encampment, where some sort of intelligence might with luck be obtained. Alone and unarmed, watched by his admiring colleagues, the little convict crossed the river and bounded away into the bush.

Graham soon picked up tracks, but his old eye was out of training and he lost them. Casting about, he observed the skins of recently eaten fruit and knew that aborigines were somewhere

* Literally "Red Beaks"—as none of the indigenous population had ever seen a white swan the colour of the beak seemed to them more significant than that of the plumage.

† This name is preserved today by the small town of Eumundi in the locality.

close at hand. It was dark when he came upon them. In the flickering light of their fires, threatening tribesmen surrounded him. Shaking spears and clubs, they would have struck him for his intrusion had not "Moilow" declared himself in their own language and divided his bread and potatoes among them.

Now welcomed to their fires, he learned that there were "two young ghosts" only a few miles away, on the opposite side of Lake Cooroibah. Graham, always quick to take advantage of a situation, claimed them as his sons, and promised hatchets and all his clothes if they would bring the "spirits" to him. A party of tribesmen, anxious to acquire such desirable items, set off in their canoes across the lake. Soon their returning lights were seen on the water and by the dim illumination of firesticks two survivors of the *Stirling Castle* were dramatically revealed. They were Robert Dayman and seventeen-year-old "Little Bob" Carey. Astonished to see his rescuer, Dayman stood rigid with surprise, while Carey threw himself on the ground thanking Heaven for his deliverance. Graham gave the naked, shivering men his jacket and shirt and, escorted by fourteen natives holding firebrands above their heads, he led the exhausted seamen back to the waiting boats.

Seeing the line of lights and hearing their distant voices, Lieutenant Otter came out to meet them, hopeful that Mrs Fraser would soon be safely in his keeping. He was disappointed to learn, after questions had been asked and answered, that she was forty miles to the north, and that Baxter, in a sorry state, was thought to be at the southern end of Great Sandy Island in the hands of a tribe who were known to be the most brutal on the coast. It seemed that they were operating in the wrong area. At Graham's suggestion one of the boats, together with seven men was despatched northwards to Double Island Point. He and Otter, with Corporal Campbell of the 4th Regiment and the convict Nathaniel Mitchell, former ploughboy and under commuted sentence of death, would walk the forty miles along the beach in the hope of gathering information on the way.

At dawn on Sunday, having generously rewarded the aborigines with six hatchets, four fishing hooks and a quantity of bread and potatoes, the little party set off hopefully northwards. The natives, anticipating more gifts, or unwilling to tear themselves away from so interesting a spectacle, followed along the clifftop until Graham, seeing that they had passed their path home, ordered them to be on their way. The aborigines, perhaps offended at this brusque treatment, suddenly changed their mood, dancing on the edge of the cliff with angry shouts and grimaces. They then began to hurl sticks, which, though thrown with force, were easily avoided. To frighten them off, Otter fired his pistol several times into the air and they retired into the woods without injury to either side. Mitchell, the ex-ploughboy, found the whole performance hilarious rather than dangerous, roaring with laughter and throwing back their missiles in return. But Graham, who knew their ways, thought it likely that they would return with rein-forcements equipped with more lethal weapons. He persuaded Otter, who had avoided bringing muskets for fear of alarming them, that with their limited armament it would be wise to return to the boat and make for Double Island Point by sea.

They rejoined the others at six o'clock that evening. Next morning, an hour before the sun rose, the indefatigable Graham, wearing nothing but his trousers and carrying a piece of bread in his waistband, set off on his second reconnaissance. In the first light of dawn, after a walk of six miles, he came upon the tracks of two aboriginal women, catching up with them as they filled their water containers in a stream. They screeched with terror at seeing him, an unrecognised "ghost" who had suddenly appeared from nowhere, but after they realised that he spoke their tongue and was alone and unarmed, they ate his bread and were soon amicably chatting with him, asking him how all their friends and relations were getting along in the "World of Spirits". He listened with more interest when they talked about a "she-ghost" in the neighbourhood. There had been a "she-ghost" and they had seen it; now it had been carried away to "*Wa-Wa*" by the men. The men had gone to a festival there and taken it with them to show to their friends!

Thus Graham learned that Mrs Fraser had been moved to the *corroboree* ground near Lake Cootharaba, known to natives as "*Wa-Wa*", "the place of crows". He was also told of a "male ghost" still alive on *Tomé** and that two others had been drowned while attempting to swim to the mainland. This was the concrete information he had been waiting for. It was a grey and sleeting day, but Graham was not deterred. Without reporting back to Lieutenant Otter, he dashed off through the dripping eucalypts to bring in Baxter from his captivity. The bold and guileful way he carried out the rescue is best told in his own words, in his account of the affair addressed to his sponsor, the Commandant at Moreton Bay†:

"Honoured Sir, you can judge my situation. Determined to fulfil my promise of bringing all those surviving people to you, and wishing to return to Mr Otter, but at the risk of life, I must fulfil the dictates of humanity, and snatch a fellow christian from a lingering state of savage brutality.

"I ran to the River about 15 miles from the boats. The blacks were all gone to fight. It rained and blew hard from the south. I walked along its banks in despair and hope, seeing no means to cross, whilst a smoke on the opposite side increased my Misery, not being able to bring them to me. About to return in despair I found a condemned canoe by which I sat and thanked my God, taking him alone to be my guard. After examining my canoe I got some stiff mud and heaped on the cracks. By the time the tide was run I was ready to buffet the waves on my sheet of Bark. This entrance is 3 Miles across, the current is so strong that Natives are doomed to wait slack water or be carried away when crossing. At 2 o'clock the tide had run and I, after hard fatigue

---

* *Tomé*, from *Tom* or "end", was the local name for the southern extremity of Great Sandy Island.

† In the interests of readability, Graham's punctuation and prose have been slightly corrected.

gained the North side, and hailed those savages who crowded from their huts and swarmed the beach to receive me as a prize.

"On my arrival their inquisitive questions detained me much, and I dreaded of ever fulfilling my promise. I enquired after my brother Spirit, which they denied at first, but after some dispute they said 'Bring him and let us see if this good ghost can speak with two tongues'. About a mile along the beach they shewed some Huts and said he was there, whilst others ran for their own sport to fetch him, when, shocking to see, the frame of a Christian Man tottering along. They would not let me go to meet him, their curiosity must be satisfied and I doomed to act in the smoothest manner to free myself from their hands. I ever must remember the emaciated form of this man, while leading through the crowd, a Skeleton of an arm extended to me, with those feeble words scarcely articulate, 'What ship, mate, did you belong?' Some time I gazed when with bursting tears saying 'I have a ship for you if God prolongs your life.'

"As it pleased them to hear us speak, I found he was the second Mate of the *Stirling Castle* by name John Baxter of the Commercial Road in London. He wished to lay down, thinking himself past recovery, and thanked God for a Christian Man to bury his body. Sinking from starvation he asked me for something to eat, at which my breast swelled and that callous heart contained therein I thought would come forth looking on those savages who said he cried. I asked them if they had any fish. Their bags were shown all empty, their bellys all hollowed-in said all was hungry. Happy moment and blest Idea which none but God could conspire at so critical a juncture, I thus retorted: 'You stand here starving while the fish are playing on the opposite shore. Your friends being gone to fight there is none to catch them. I found a whale at 'Gullirae' (Double Island Point) and I came to tell him and you, knowing he was hungry.'

"The bags were brought to carry the whale and the nets to catch the fish—and in about an hour landed 8 canoes with 18 blacks, my brother spirit and myself. Assisting him all I could with every kind of hope, having brought him from the most brutal blacks along the coast. They kept looking for Fish, and often going to turn and bring me with them. I kept urging them on, the sun going down, when the Almighty God sent a shoal of Bream—they instantly surrounded and caught some of them. This caused me to rally and them to believe. They caught several after, which confirmed everything I said. My comrade, who I was heartening on holding firebrands before him,* told me I must make his Grave, he could go no further, his death was inevitable.

"The blacks must fill their bellies and sleep till morning. It was now dark, and seeing I could not carry nor yet leave him, I was forced through humanity to break my promise though determined to fulfil it. Having made a fire and pulled a bed of grass for him on which he sat while the Blacks roasted their Fish of which he got some bits. I got one Bream, I eat the head of it, he the rest. Keeping a fire by him all night I was doomed to keep them in conversation. Seeing the necessity of getting him something to eat I hurried them off about 3 o'clock on Tuesday Morning. They were to stop about 3 miles ahead and us to follow them at daylight.

"Three old men and a girl stayed with us. I left him in their charge to bring him with them, while I went to the Womens Camp again lest this Lady might be concealed. I surprised them at the break of day. She was not there. My diligence was all in vain. Returning in despair I was consoled at finding my ward seated among some Blacks eating Fish. They having caught more than they could eat, throwing me some, their bellies being full and wanting to have sport. I here threw off the mask seeing the whale was of no use for men that had more than they wanted. Wishing to hurry them along I told them I had left two canoes at 'Gullirae' with Tomahawks to get them honey, and plenty of Honey which I and my fellow spirits had brought, who were all

* Graham was holding a firebrand above Baxter's heart in order to improve his circulation.

83

their friends, and naming several Blacks, men who were dead, and assuring them they were there. They must come and see. Thus, I decoyed and got myself from amongst them.

"I had now six miles to go and my ward having his belly full, the first since he came amongst them, wanted less of my assistance. I, having a more serious undertaking, if one there could be, pursued the diverting fancy of those about me; he whom I freed coming on at leisure. Coming in sight of the tents I was met by Mr Otter, who thinking the Lady might be amongst the crowd that surrounded me, brought some necessaries of Dress for her, but what was his disappointment and apprehension of horror for that suffering female when I gave him a description of where and how she was carried to be the show and mock of wild savages upwards of forty miles from where we were. He was a little consoled when I told him I got the mate, and then coming on, he said the savages had caused them to remove their Tent, and they were forced to Fire in defence. He expressed his sincere concern in behalf of me, giving me the wardrobe to proceed to the Tents, he hurried to the assistance of the mate who was then in sight. The Blacks I caused to sit 100 yards or more from the tents, and were brought 6 Tomahawks, a Bucket of Water sweetened as syrup, with Bread and potatoes. The girl, a child of 6 years of age, I brought to the camp, put my shirt on it, knowing her father was 'Bully' and might hear of it. Mr Otter gave it a handkerchief. The Natives were surprised and pleased at seeing ghosts from the world of Spirits. I was now in consternation how to proceed and free that forlorn Lady from a lingering death."

Thus Baxter was saved from starvation. Despite the generous gift of food and tomahawks, his hosts seemed sad to lose him and wailed "Curri! Curri!" as they left the camp of their island home.

Last on the rescue list was the greatest prize of all. Graham now had confirmation that Mrs Fraser was living out her nightmare at the *corroboree* ground on Lake Cootharaba, forty miles to the south, only a short distance from where he had saved

Dayman and Carey. To be sure of his freedom Graham knew that he must bring her in. He made his plan: he was to go alone, but Lieutenant Otter was to follow down the beach with an armed party to a spot Graham would mark in the sand. Without wasting any time the convict, who should reasonably have been exhausted by his earlier efforts, set off at a steady lope southwards. In his description of his dangerous adventure, the little Irishman casts himself in an almost heroic mould; Captain Foster Fyans, reading his statement in leisure back at base, must have felt gratified that his man had in no way let him down.

"Your Honor to whom I here refer—the difficulties I had to surmount, the horrors of Death which to me seemed sure, and even prophesied by my Comrades who were praying for my safety, and vowed to have revenge for my blood, expecting to see me no more. I was determined to brave the worst of fates or finish a miserable existence to rescue that abject captive Lady.

"Though solicited by that Gentleman Mr Otter to accompany me with all the arms he had, it was of no avail, for had we been able to assail them she must have fallen a sacrifice to their spears or be carried by hundreds further through the mountains. I must act on other plans though doomed to face hundreds of savages, amongst whom were the very men who but a few days before were fired at. I depended on a tribe whose former friendship I had experienced, several of whom acknowledged me their Father, or spirit there-of. There were several resolutions of detaining Hostages and sending word, to see if they would give her up. This would have caused lives on both sides, and certainly would have proved fatal to her and also shewn a coward in me, I alone knowing where she was. I think it a pleasure in giving your Honor an account of this transaction and every minute detail, shewing I was determined, or die the worst of deaths, to fulfil my promise.

"Lieut. Otter wishing to accompany me, I spoke these words: "Sir, I am but one, my life I care not for, it being of little use to me. If I do not return in two days then take hostages and revenge for my blood.' He took me to his tent giving me a glass of rum and water. I here gave him directions of the route. He was to follow me on the following morning to the mark of the broad arrow which I was to leave for his instruction, and to sit where it was, stop till I should come next day if living. I strove much to get 2 of those Blacks to come with me. I brought them to the tents, shewed 2 Blankets, 2 Tomahawks and 2 axes to induce them to come. They told me their hearts failed them, they would be killed. I recollect telling Mr Otter at the time what they said, when taking a roasted bream and a small piece of bread I took my departure, my comrades saying they would revenge my fate, expecting no more to see me. I soon crossed the hills and was out of sight on Tuesday at 11 o'clock August the 16th.

"Lest my bread should be took from me, expecting to meet several natives, I eat it. I had trousers on, and continued my route making the mark as I went along. Drawing near sundown I thought of my supper, having none and no time to look for any. Your Honor can here read Ideas of my mind, and think the arm of God alone strengthened and assisted me in this virtuous act of humanity. Proceeding on, I found a snake 7 feet long which shewed providence was assisting and protecting me. On getting back I retired to a gully, and made a fire and roasted my snake which I hung up for morning. Of all my life this was the most disturbed night I ever spent, too tedious to mention here. The dawn of day called me forth, after taking God for my guide, and my breakfast which his mercies sent me.

"I descended from my gully 25 miles from the Tents and continued my route, making the Mark. On coming where I was to turn I put a stop with those words 'Stop Here You will find fresh water at the rock'. This was 30 miles in all. I saw no Blacks ascending the hills and crossing the Forest ground. About 4 miles you descend into a boggy ground or swamp ankle deep for a mile, after which a lake about 30 miles in circumference,* 4 miles where I crossed it, knee deep at low water, after which a fresh water River.

* Lake Cootharaba.

86

"Being about to swim across, a Black man and his wife appeared in their canoe, being horror struck at my appearance and thinking I had more confederates they were making away saying they would bring plenty of men. I standing on the brink of the River telling them I was alone, and shewing 2 Fish hooks, the woman induced him to return. Their approach was timid, and he asking what he would get. I tore a leg off my trousers and gave it to him. The hooks to her. After inquiring the different tribes that were there, and particularly after my own kindred, and what part of the field they were in, I made enquiry after my wife, (the woman who said I was her Husband's spirit and died in 1827), if she had strayed amongst them. They told me there was a female spirit there, but a man by the name of 'Mothervane' claimed her as his wife's sister. They had heard of the skirmages we had, which I left to the stupid spirits which were along with me, and said I came to do no harm but take my wife down to the beach and there live on my own ground as I had done before. I promised him my trousers, and her as many hooks as she could carry, if she would go and tell the men, especially my friends, not to be cross as I came to live amongst them and make axes and Fish hooks at 'Thaying' (the name of the ground that belonged to me), and I would show 'Mothervane' that spirit was 'Mamba', whose sons were there—'Murrow Dooling' and 'Caravanty', two young men who always claimed me as their Father's spirit, who had a great connection in several tribes. The woman said they were there and I despatched her to tell them, while the man and I hurried on telling me he would assist me.

"On coming in sight of the camp, I watched the woman going to the south side where I supposed my friends were. I was making onward, but, surrounded by numbers, I was forced to stand. Black and savage as they were, no horror struck me so much as the sight of that unhappy Lady, who caught my eye as it wandered round their Huts. Could I then have armed myself with vengeance would I have been detained from giving the Cannibal race any account of my demands? Courage flushed to me and I feared no fate. Hearing the sound of 'Mamba', which the woman had been told she was, and my sons amongst the crowd, to whom I said: 'Is your eyes blind, don't you know your Mother,' upon who's neck I fell, fancying to cry. My father-in-law 'Mootemu' jumped to his knife, saying, 'no crying, go and take her.' Upwards of 400 Blacks had seized their spears when 'Mothervane' came forward, to whom I said, 'Do you claim a Spirit? and she my Wife. She can't speak to tell having lost her speech, and I who have got sense do tell the truth and here are her two sons and Father', pointing to the people above-named. A dead silence was here and all eyes were on me whilst I told them how she was along with me in a canoe after Turtle, and being cast away she swam against the North men, who gave her nothing to eat, she being a stranger could not tell who were her friends, having lost her tongue, and if 'Mothervane' would be cross I would call a challenge. Here throwing off my trousers, to make fresh friends, I impeached them with being stupid in not knowing her. All the coast Blacks here stood on my side, and said I always told the truth, saying 'give her', 'she is his', being now satisfied that she was 'Mamba'. Yet they wanted me to go with them into the mountains as their friends had heard of that spirit and their hearts would be glad at seeing her. I here said: 'You see she is near dead with hunger, let your friends wait till she is recovered and then I will go a season to the Mountains.' 'Mothervane' said it was a pity to let the Spirit go, but here 'Mootemu' said, 'they are 2 ghosts and no men has any rights to separate them. "Moilow" has good sense and knows how to live as well as us, he must have his wife.' The father of the child to whom I had given the shirt coming forward, telling him what I had done for his girl, and where I left her with a full belly, not as my wife was, starving among them. He said in an angry voice: 'You people hear that, he is coming with good fingers and why be cross.'

"They began to retire to their respective huts, and a Black man sitting opposite her hut, and again I seen the face of a Christian Woman, and a Black man sitting opposite her hut with a spear in his hand as a Centinal. On looking I recognised him to be the nephew of mine who has four wives, by name 'Dapen' and coming to me said 'come uncle I was watching my Aunt; that the Mountain Blacks should not come near, whilst you were talking. Fear none. I'll give her to you.' On approaching the Hut, could I believe I lost my sense with surprise and joy, and a sense of gratitude to most of those savages who stood my friends. With a heartfelt sorrow for her then before me, I sunk to the ground. When roused by the voice of 'Dapen' saying 'The sun is going round uncle, you have far to go.' Roused to a sense of my situation I rose and reached out my hand to her, saying 'Come with me. God has made me your deliverer.'

"This Lady rising and taking my hand, I proceeded through a camp of some hundreds of Blacks. On the most judicious plan I asked four of those men to come with me to 'Nemberthan'. Taking my leave of my friends, 'Mootemu' wanted me to take some 'Bungwal' (a root) which I refused. Having come to the canoes, two were brought—three in each we crossed the lake. On her head was a South-wester, the smell of paint kept the Blacks from taking it. Around her loins were part of the legs and waist-band of a pair of trousers, which covered part of her thighs, wound round with Vines twenty fold as well for delicacy as the preservation of her marriage and earrings which she concealed under the Vines, and the only articles that were saved from those savage hands.

"In ascending the Forest ground I caused the Blacks to follow my example which they did to the rocks, where arriving I saw that relief was come. Leaving the Lady at the water hole telling her to remain a few minutes, I took the Blacks along with me to the beach where was Lieut. Otter who came to meet me in such haste that almost frightened the Blacks, enquiring where she was. I told him all was right, asking him for some clothes for her, at which he clasped his hands and thanked his God, going to his bag. I seated the Blacks along with Corporals McGuire and Campbell of the 4th Regiment and Nathaniel Mitchell who came with Mr Otter, to whom I went and got a boat cloak and some other articles of dress and returned to prepare the Lady for his reception, and for the first time them vines were pulled off which the hands of her dear and much lamented husband had put on. I beg leave to omit several distressing incidents in regard to this surprising unhappy Lady whose history of woes is unparalleled as also in passing any encomiums in behalf of myself through the many acts I was destined to fulfil under the providence of God. Your Honor best can judge the situation of her mind, being about to enter Society, and the distress which attended this meeting when assisting her forth I gave her hand to that gentleman Mr Otter about 1 O'clock on Wednesday 17th of August".

Such was Graham's poetic account of the rescue. There is also on record a powerful description of Mrs Fraser's arrival at the rendezvous seen through the eyes of Lieutenant Otter.*

"After we had gone about thirty miles we came to a mark in the sand, the signal agreed upon for us to stop and wait for him. We had not been here half an hour, when Graham appeared with four natives on the top of the cliff above us. When he came down the hill, the blacks, on seeing us armed, attempted to run away, but he persuaded them by promises of hatchets to turn back. I went up to meet him, and you may conceive my joy and satisfaction when he told me that Mrs Fraser was waiting on the top of the hill until I sent her a cloak, I immediately gave him a cloak and petticoat, and shortly afterwards she appeared. You never saw such an object. Although only thirty-eight years of age, she looked like an old woman of seventy, perfectly black, and dreadfully crippled from the sufferings she had undergone. I went to meet her, and she caught my hand, burst into tears, and sunk down quite exhausted. She was a mere skeleton, the skin literally hanging upon her bones, whilst her legs were a mass of sores, where the savages had tortured her with firebrands. Notwithstanding her miserable plight, it was absolutely necessary for us to start homewards, though she had already come nine or ten

* In a letter to his sister in England (September 1836).

miles, as there were about 300 natives in the camp, who, Graham said, would most likely attack us in the night, for many of them had been unwilling to give her up. He had fortunately met with one of his former friends, a kind of chief, through whose influence he had succeeded. So treacherous are the natives, that it is impossible to trust one of them for a moment.

"After having given the poor woman some port wine, which I had brought with me in a flask, and some tea, which she thought was nectar from heaven, she insisted upon immediately setting out, though we had nearly thirty miles to walk. On the road she gave me a dismal account of her hardships and privations, interrupting herself with bursts of gratitude, which it was painful to listen to."

Mrs Fraser's feet were in a shocking state. Someone at the *corroboree* ground had stuck a spear into her ankle and it had swollen so much that she could only hop with difficulty on the arm of Lieutenant Otter. Soon she could hardly walk at all and had to be carried on the shoulders of the aborigines who still accompanied them. In this fashion, they loped along at a steady trot until they were within eight miles of the base camp. Otter ordered Graham to go ahead and prepare for her reception. The aborigines, seeing their friend and protector leave them, cried that without him they would be shot, and immediately ran into the bush in terror. Alternately hopping and being carried by the soldiers, Mrs Fraser finally reached the boats at Double Island Point at three o'clock in the morning on Thursday the 18th of August.

X

Back At Moreton Bay

Though her captivity was over, Mrs Fraser found no security on gaining the waiting boats. As had been anticipated, the aborigines pursued them and seemed intent on getting her back into their possession. They would have realised they had been duped and no doubt bitterly resented their white friend's deception, and the loss of their slave and prize exhibit. The boats urgently put out to sea, but bad weather forced them back; the long cold wait on the beach before the party could sail was graphically described in notes recorded by Foster Fyans:

"The night was fast approaching, a heavy sea and blowing strong from the south with occasional rain. Experiencing constant annoyance from the multitude of natives then assembled, and hourly their numbers increasing, the party remained close on the beach, wet cold and miserable, fires were not permitted. The natives incurred so much leniency they became bold and daring, as occasionally during the night to come within the camp in hope to pilfer, a jacket or an old cap by them was considered a prize of no small value. Some were seized in the act, but still the same forbearance and leniency existed. A constant riot was kept up during the night, yelling, with an occasional Boomerang on fire thrown over the camp by the natives, many of the Boomerangs so skillfully handled, an art so perfectly understood by the Aborigines, that often passing through the air twice, or thrice, over the party returned to the spot where it was thrown from. The natives, during the progress of this strange instrument, felt great joy, particularly when the flame afforded them sufficient light to see the party. Only one accident occurred during the

night from the Boomerang, old Sandy, as named in the settlement, had his jaw broken. Another poor fellow received a spear,
it passed through his chest, and out of his back, he died immediately, and a third of the party was severely wounded by a
spear experiencing painful agony for weeks, when death released
him. The night passed away without a single shot having been fired.

"Providence is good. The morning broke fine, a favourable
change of wind to the south cheered the party, fires blazing, camp
kettles set on with innumerable pannicans of tea to boil, then to
work for the sea.

"The boats all ready for launching, water smooth, the natives
perceiving the preparations began closing, the men standing to
their arms, again advanced and fell back. Repeating this several
times when it was advisable to shove no. 1 and no. 6 boats into
the sea, to anchor as close as possible, the crews to be in readiness
to receive the natives in the event of a rush. Mrs Fraser was
placed in no. 2, all ready, each crew at their own boat. The word
given, off my hearties, running the four* boats into the sea,
jumping in. This movement so paralysed the natives, not one
moved. At last when the oars splashed, the loud voices *Wa, Wa,*
sounded on the cliffs, the crews gave three hearty cheers making
a straight course for the Brisbane, the natives kept the shore for
many miles with shout after shout more particularly when the
boats assembled in a cluster to perform the last ceremony over
their departed comrade."

With the last "*Wa, Wa*" fading behind them anxieties vanished
and the two-day journey home was all "plain sailing". Mrs Fraser
sitting in the stern with Lieutenant Otter at her side, could not
stop talking; the convict crew were in rollicking form at the
success of the venture and the hope of remission, singing sea-
shanties and being more familiar with the "diamonds" than was
usually tolerated.†

* Fyans, whose memory was apt to be flighty, seems to have made an
error in the number of boats, and to have exaggerated the injuries to the men.

† The red-coated soldiers were known as "diamonds" on account of the
pattern made by their white leather accoutrements.

Back at Moreton Bay, everyone turned out to meet them, and Mrs Fraser, who had made pathetic efforts to improve her appearance en route, was an object of immense interest to all. She was bustled off to the house of Stephen Owen, head of the Commissariat department, where his wife Bridget and her female convict housemaids had some difficulty in "cleaning-up" their visitor. Having shorn off most of her matted hair they "poulticed her from head to foot" in the hope that new skin might replace the old. She was feverish and confused, rambling on about her experience in a manner that pained and embarrassed her listeners. Dr Robertson, who attended her, reported that she was obsessed with the idea that she was pregnant, but he was finally able to convince her that this was not the case. The rest of the survivors went into hospital, where they were mortified to be denied, in the interest of their health, all meat for several days and confined to a diet of arrow-root and sago. Nevertheless Baxter appears soon to have recovered his strength and became an "out-patient" at the house of Colour Sergeant Parry of Lieutenant Otter's regiment.

Captain Foster Fyans had given the convict crew a good dinner and promised them that though he personally had no authority to give them remission he would forward their names to the Governor at Sydney, Sir Richard Bourke, with a strong recommendation. He was gratified to find that not one article was missing from the stores and that even the four bottles of wine included for Mrs Fraser had been returned intact.

What had been the reactions of Darge and Youlden, who throughout this time had been hanging around the settlement, when confronted with the emergent "she-captain" who could have little good to say about them? Certainly she denounced them—Captain Foster Fyans, in a report to the Colonial Secretary at Sydney, expressed his own stern judgement:—

"I am happy to state that since Mrs Fraser's arrival she has improved in health, and also the crew; some were very weakly from constant exposure to the weather and being without food for months—on the statement of this lady regarding the conduct of the Sailors, I consider that they have been the cause of the loss of the lives of Capt. Fraser and Mr Brown the first mate— no doubt can exist if the men did their duty and obeyed the Captain's orders, the Boat would have reached our Pilot Station as Mr Brown perfectly knew the place (Mr Bryant, the Agent for the Ship is aware of this, and is to see how far the men are punishable). However, as the parties will be forwarded to Sydney by the first ship, I refer the case for His Excellency's consideration and do myself the honour to forward the statements of Mrs Fraser and Mr Baxter the second Mate.

"The general conduct and manner of Robert Darge, Harry Youlden and Robert Dayman since their arrival has been disrespectful and bad, and an apparent unwillingness on the parts of the first two to give any information regarding Captain Fraser and his lady I beg to state that they arrived here long previous to Mrs Fraser and regret to say they enjoyed every kindness and hospitality, but on hearing her statement I immediately dislodged them from our quarters, appointed them a single room in the barracks and provided them with the ration No. 5 which I consider is much more than their past conduct merits."

True to his word, he sent a letter off to Government House, Sydney, giving a good report on the protagonists:—

Sir,

In obedience to the commands of His Excellency the Governor, I do myself the honor to enclose a list of the names and particulars of the party of prisoners, composing the boat's crew, sent under the Command of Lieutenant Otter in search of the Shipwrecked crew of the Brig Stirling Castle; *and upon a reference to that gentleman, I am happy to say, that no distinction can be made in the exemplary conduct of the whole party, and therefore recommend them as generally worthy of His Excellency's notice. Notwithstanding their degraded state as convicts the willingness evinced on their parts was a pleasure to witness.*

With respect to John Graham he having only until next May to serve when he will become entirely free, I hope His Excellency will consider him entitled to a greater share of indulgence than the others, and direct his return to Head Quarters by the next Vessel. From the intelligence and firmness displayed by this man, I am certain should His Excellency at any future period think a survey of the North Coast advisable, Graham would be a most useful man in the undertaking.

I have the honor to be,
Sir,
Your most obedient servant,
Foster Fyans
Capt. 4th Regt.
Comdt.

Foster Fyans paid Mrs Fraser a visit in her sick-room, which he described in his Reminiscences: "She looked better, and most contented, but in a few seconds broke out, prostrating herself on the floor, blessing me for the paper.* It was evident the poor soul was mentally a sufferer." The second time he visited her he found her "stronger in mind". She haltingly related some past events: "The sad death of her husband, Mr Brown the mate and others of the crew who died from the severe treatment. She said the Waddy was bad enough, but the firestick is awful. Mr Brown, so long as his health continued, the blacks were fond of him, he worked so well, always seeking their good will in the hope of escaping. After some months wandering in nakedness he lost his strength, the blacks began to persecute him, to make him keep up with the tribe. A firestick would be applied, when he decreased on the application, perhaps another which always caused great merriment. Mr Brown was a mass of ulcers caused chiefly by the firestick. He died close to the water but unable to get to it. His

* The "paper" referred to was a letter he had written to establish the "bona fides" of its bearer. Surprisingly Graham does not mention it in his report of the rescue.

Mrs Fraser, from *Shipwreck Of The Stirling Castle*, John Curtis, 1838.

A government gaol gang, Sydney, New South Wales, from A. Earle's *Views In New South Wales And Van Dieman's Land*, 1830.

The wreck of the
Stirling Castle, from
*Shipwreck Of The
Stirling Castle*,
John Curtis, 1838.

Mrs Fraser in search of water, from *Shipwreck Of The Stirling Castle*, John Curtis, 1838.

The arrival of the aborigines, from a contemporary print.

Mrs Fraser being fought over by rival
claimants, from *Narrative Of The
Capture, Sufferings And Miraculous
Escape Of Mrs. Eliza Fraser*, Charles
Webb, New York, 1837.

Mrs Fraser and the crew of the Stirling
Castle assaulted by aborigines, from *Shipwreck
Of Mrs. Fraser And Loss Of The Stirling
Castle,* Dean & Munday, 1837.

The spearing of Captain Fraser, from *Shipwreck Of The Stirling Castle*, John Curtis, 1838.

Aborigines at home, from a contemporary print.

Aborigines fishing, from a contemporary print.

An aborigine mother and child, from a contemporary print.

An aboriginal hunting scene, from a contemporary print.

John Baxter.

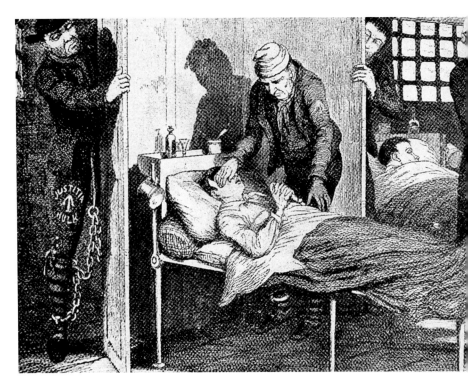

A sketch depicting convict life, from
A Complete Exposure Of The Convict System

Death of a convict in a prison hulk, from a drawing by George Cruikshank.

Mrs Fraser's escape from the savages, from *Shipwreck Of The Stirling Castle*, John Curtis, 1838.

last day was beyond description. Here she became agitated, saying 'I see him before me, and my poor husband.' I begged of her to be composed, and never again to relate any of these unfortunate events. She promised to do so. I informed her of the Governor's intended kindness, and her proposed departure for Sydney by the Government Schooner which was expected hourly. Rather dissatisfaction appeared in her by this information—she said, 'I have none known to me in Sydney, I now wish I had even died the death of my husband.' Remonstrating with her, suggesting a speedy return to England, where I hoped she would meet her family and friends, her thoughts brightened, at once coming to the determination, quickly putting the question: 'On what day am I to embark?' 'That rests in yourself,' I replied, 'you must prepare your trunks, and regulate.' 'I have nothing.' 'You are wrong, Mrs Fraser. There are two large chests of things for you, all your own property, also a purse from your friends in Moreton Bay, and on your arrival in Sydney, I feel assured that the good Governor, and his amiable daughter Mrs Thompson will obtain a passage to England for you.' She expressed great feelings of gratitude."

The good Commandant, who seemed to have the impression that he alone had effected the rescue of the *Stirling Castle* survivors, then occupied himself with the question of their ultimate disposal. He ordered the settlement's cutter, the *Regent Bird*, to Sydney with a report to the Governor and a request for a vessel appropriate for transporting Mrs Fraser. The cutter returned with word that the *Prince George* would be available in the middle of the month. Captain Fyans gave an amusingly patronising account of his small navy's execution of its mission:

"Having taken the responsibility of acting as I have represented I felt more than anxious to make my immediate report to the Government. The *Regent Bird* cutter, commanded by Mr King our admiral, was ordered to be in readiness. She sailed. On their arrival at Sydney, to the great disgust of our proud Admiral, he was boarded by a Man of War boat, and not treated handsomely.

The pride of his heart and soul—his fine flowing pendant—hauled down, his noble flag shared the same fate. He was severely admonished for such presumption. He delivered his despatches, causing the greatest possible interest, not failing to lay his charge of piracy before the Governor, who must have smiled as he interested himself, and under existing circumstances caused the flags to be restored. In a few hours the despatches were delivered on board. Immediate, the Admiral's blue peter up and gun fired. He was a proud old man—on making his report to me of the treatment he had received in Sydney he became excited, explaining that 'a boy, a midshipman, boarded me, robbing me of my flags, threatened to eat me up, and would so do he said, if he had a bit of salt in his pocket. I have served the Government for nearly forty years, in command of the *Regent* for the last ten, and to be treated so is more than a joke.' 'Well', said I, 'King, you have your flags, and keep them. When you fall in with a Man of War never sport pendants, but you can do as you please.' He smiled saying, 'I cut it as thick as bricks Captain, I sailed past the brig of war in full blossom, I sported all my flags.' "

It was seven weeks before the *Prince George*, sent up to take them to Sydney, arrived at Moreton Bay. She anchored off the sandbanks at the Pilot Station, and boats of the settlement, manned as usual by convicts, rowed down on the ebbing tide. A contemporary account gives a rich description of their send-off:—

"Every thing being arranged for a final separation, Baxter, Corallis, Carey (the boy), Dayman, Youlden and Darge, embarked in a whale-boat, manned with eight men at the oars, and a helmsman, in order to proceed down the river to the *Prince George* cutter. They started about eleven o'clock, am; and Mrs Fraser and the lady of Dr Robinson,* with her domestic attendant, together with Lieutenant Otter, entered a skiff about three pm, the vessel being manned with scientific steersmen, etc.; and although numerically considered, a diminutive crew, yet the

* The settlement doctor was in fact Dr Kinnear Robertson.

parties composing it were well versed in the knowledge of the sub-marine pinnacles which had their base between the settlement and the bar to the Bay; and thus by manoeuvre they reached 'Point Look-Out' nearly as soon as the whale-boat, whose greater draught of water caused them to take a more zig-zag course.

"The brave captain of the *Prince George*, who had been sent from Sydney for the purpose already named, having received information by the crew and passengers of the whale-boat that more distinguished visitors would shortly arrive; with 'the heart of a true British sailor' he prepared for their reception and accommodation; and although on their arrival they were not saluted by 'fire and smoke', they were hailed with hearty exclamations of welcome, and regaled with as elegant and substantial *déjeuner à la fourchette* as could be expected in the cabin of a revenue cutter.

"The assemblage of this trio of vessels we should have been delighted to have beheld. What a congress! What congratulations and confabulations too! Moreover, what an heterogenous mixture of character! There stood the heroine of our history, as one rescued almost by miracle from the grasp of brutal men, with every eye fixed upon her, and every eye sparkled that gazed. Although in a physical point of view she was partially recovered, yet she was still 'haggard, poor, and lean', and bearing evident marks of the tortures which she had undergone, and of the degrading disfigurement to which her person had been subjected by the hand of ferocious barbarity.

"There stood Lieutenant Otter like a brave champion, and his eyes flashed in those of the captain of the *Prince George* with a conscious but unassuming pride—and well he might!

"After mutual congratulations had been interchanged, the captain of the cutter requested a detail of the sufferings of the party he was delegated to take charge of. Lieutenant Otter became the spokesman, and gave a recital which caused the captain to list with the taciturnity of a dumb spectator.

"The gallant officer pointed to the lady he had rescued, and with a look of pride blended with compassion, he entered into a succinct detail of her sufferings; and, as far as delicacy would permit, the insults which she had undergone.

"At length the time arrived when Lieutenant Otter must retrograde to the settlement, and the *Prince George* proceed on her voyage; and the friends parted, never more, perhaps, to meet again. It appears to us, from the expressions of the narrators, that they will ever have a grateful and lively recollection of the numerous acts of kindness which they received at Moreton Bay —indeed, gratitude demands that it should be so, and they never ought to cease to pray for their welfare. Any change or movement which would carry them toward their natal land, neutralised the pangs of separation. Exiled as they had been, and sufferers as they were, they could feelingly exclaim with our favourite poet, 'England, with all thy faults, I love thee still'."

XI

The News Reaches Sydney

It so happened that news of the loss of the *Stirling Castle* had already reached Sydney from another source. On August 10th, the day before the rescue expedition set out from Moreton Bay, the schooner *Nancy* arrived from Port Macquarie, the former penal station situated midway between the two. On board was a bedraggled passenger, none other than "Middle Bob", Robert Hodge, only survivor of the pinnace party which had ruthlessly sailed away from the reef leaving their shipmates in the sinking long-boat.

Hodge's story, and there was none present to refute it, told how they had missed the long-boat during the night and had diligently but unsuccessfully searched for it before deciding to make their way to Moreton Bay to summon help. He described how the pinnace had later broken up on the coral while landing for water, forcing them to continue on foot. They never got to Moreton Bay. Having no navigational instruments, they had failed to realise that they had sailed past the entrance to the river and in fact made their landfall a hundred miles to the south. Thus, they had unwittingly walked in the direction of Sydney, at least four hundred miles away.

According to Hodge a succession of disasters had overtaken the members of his party. Young John Fraser, the captain's nephew, had been the first to go—drowned while collecting shellfish from a rock. John Wilson, the other cabin boy, had also drowned under circumstances which Hodge did not elaborate. He claimed that Stone, the bosun, and Schofield, the carpenter, had come to grief while crossing the wide Clarence River—local aborigines had taken them in canoes to an island in the middle and would not let them continue until they had been rewarded with waistcoats. Refusal had led to the sailors being speared and left to die. Allan, the coloured cook, had apparently fallen exhausted in the bush about fifteen miles north of the McCleay River, and James Major was thought to have been burned and eaten by natives.

Behind Hodge's halting tale of misadventure there could have been more sinister happenings. It was not unknown for men in desperate straits to kill and eat their companions—there are a number of macabre cases on record of escaped convicts starving in the bush and killing each other one by one to the number of five and six (Appendix II). Were there unspeakable secrets behind Hodge's laconic account? It can be imagined that the tender boys were first to go and the gradual diminution of the rest of the party may have been attended by horrific confrontations.

Hodge must have felt some alarm when he learned that several of the long-boat party had lived to tell their tale, and doubly anxious when Captain Roach of the revenue cutter *Prince George*, sent to Moreton Bay to bring the survivors back to Sydney, was given orders by the governor to see if any of the pinnace party might still be alive. On his way back from his mission to Moreton Bay Captain Roach, following up his instructions, landed in the area where Hodge had been rescued and was soon to come upon a grisly remnant. Curtis, who had the story from Baxter, described the occasion in his graphically fulsome style:—

"The cutter had not sailed more than a hundred miles before the crew saw a number of fires on or near the beach; and owing to the stillness of the water and a slight breeze, Baxter could easily distinguish the boisterous *coo-eeing* of the natives, a proof that they were in one of their merriest moods. Captain Roach consulted those who had a painful experience of the manners of the barbarians, and was advised to keep out from the shores until day-break, because if any of the missing crew were in their hands, intimidation arising from the approach of an armed cutter might cause the natives to hurry the captives further into the bush, or perhaps at once destroy them.

"Perhaps we may both be accused of uncharitable feeling when we candidly express that the narrators felt a repugnance at nearing the shore, lest they should become victims to the fatal and un-erring spear, or again be taken into captivity; if this were so, it partakes not of cowardice, but emanates from the strong inherent principle in our nature—self-preservation.

"Be this as it may, Captain Roach had his prescribed orders, and like a brave and obedient commander, he followed them up to the very letter. On the following morning he proceeded to the beach, and with his crew went on shore. The natives had retired into the bush, and all was silence save the muttering of the rippling ocean, and the warbling of the splendidly fledged birds which abound in that latitude. Sounds were echoed, which would have been well defined had they reached an European ear, but no one approached. They had not proceeded far along the coast near the sea shore, ere their attention was attracted by the impress of human feet on the earth. These the enterprising party followed until they came to a spot where it was evident a recent corrobery had been held. It was not long before one of the crew sounded the alarm, which caused all his companions to fly to the spot from whence the sound proceeded. On their arrival, they beheld their companion rivetted to the spot in a state approaching petri-fication; and no wonder, for his eyes were fixed upon the dis-figured body and extremities of a person who has already been named in this narrative—they were the remains of James Major!

"It appeared, from small fragments of bones which lay near his disfigured trunk, that the natives had placed his head on a fire, which consumed the thorax, and descended obliquely to a part of the left side of the abdomen, when it appeared to have satiated its vengeance, or perhaps its flame was extinguished by the gushing of the heart's blood of the victim! From appearances, it was calculated that the sacrifice had been made two or three days before the landing of our exploring party; and, but for a comparatively trivial circumstance at first view, it would never have been known who the sufferer had been, or to what nation he belonged. Baxter, Darge, and others of the rescued, were conveyed to the spot, when, with one voice, they proclaimed that it was their late shipmate, Major. And how did they identify him? It was thus: From some cause or other, the sanguinary brutes who put him to death, had either from forgetfulness, or that their rapacity was blunted by a deed of bloodshed, failed to denude him of a well-known waistcoat, the colour and remaining buttons of which were recognized by Baxter and his companions. We have already stated the progress which the fire had made upon the disfigured and headless corpse. But the work of destruction did not end here,—it was quite apparent that the kangaroo dogs had made a hearty meal on the most fleshy part of the thighs and legs of the poor fellow, so that what remained of him was a horrid spectacle to behold. Well might the first discoverer have been petrified; for even when relating the particulars to us for the purpose of narration, Baxter's flesh quivered as though he had been torn by pincers, and made the blood of the author curdle in the veins. When describing Major's aptitude as a seaman, and descanting upon the good qualities of his unfortunate defunct friend, the tear of the sailor, than which we think nothing is more affecting, gushed from his lashes—a tear, we doubt not, excited by gratitude combined with regret—gratitude for his own preservation—regret for the fate of his companions."

Baxter's lurid story of the eating of James Major, or at least Curtis's interpretation of it, seems over-imaginative or naïve. Had the aborigines made a meal of Major it is highly unlikely that they would have done the job incompletely and wasted so important a piece of protein as his remaining flesh, or abandoned so desirable an object as his waistcoat with gilt buttons. It is more likely that either Hodge murdered him and partially ate him, or more probably he met with an accident while sleeping in a deserted shelter, which caught fire during the night. As Doctor Lang, writing about the customs of the natives ("Cooksland",

1848) has observed, "From their manner of living, and especially from their always having a fire burning on the bare ground in front of their miserable huts, close to where they sleep, they are peculiarly liable to accidents from fire. Their feet are often burned severely and often other parts of their bodies."

Whatever the cause of death, the remains of James Major were buried then and there, and as much as could be remembered by Captain Roach of the burial service read over him. The *Prince George* then continued toward Sydney where she arrived on October 15th.

Mrs Fraser was installed at the house of the colonial secretary, Mr Thompson. She was treated as something of a celebrity and, now apparently recovered, was to be seen at many tea parties and picnics around the town. Though competing with belated reports of the scandalous divorce action in London involving Caroline Norton and Lord Melbourne, her story was printed at length in the local papers and included details that may have been products of a heated imagination. The wind was to some extent taken out of her sails by the presence in Sydney at that time of two survivors of the *Charles Eaton*, also wrecked on the Barrier Reef. Their story was almost more dramatic than hers—having "adopted" a passenger's four-year-old son William D'Oyley, and the ship's boy John Ireland, the natives had murdered fourteen of the survivors and had artistically arranged their skulls to decorate a totem. It is known that Mrs Fraser was introduced to the two boys at the house of Mr Slade of the Board of Commissioners, but there is no record of their conversation.

The citizens of Sydney were generous in their attentions. A special service was held for the *Stirling Castle* survivors at St James's Church, designed by the convict Francis Greenaway, where the Episcopalian Bishop of Australia, who then came under the direction of the Archbishop of Madras, preached a Thanksgiving sermon which made frequent use of nautical metaphor. Mrs Fraser, who was having trouble with her joints, did not feel well enough to attend; but the rest of the seamen, with the exception of Hodge, who was lame, were there, and to their embarrassment were made to sit in the aisle without their jackets, presumably to recreate something of the "spirit of shipwreck" and excite the generosity of the congregation whose collection money was supposedly for their welfare. Whatever the amount given, and later forthcoming by public subscription, the crew saw nothing of it and benefited only by the gift of some second-hand clothes. Baxter complained to Mr Bryant, agent for the owners of the *Stirling Castle*, and asked to see the subscription list. He was told that this was not possible but that particulars would in due course be published in the local press.* Possibly Mrs Fraser was considered the only deserving member of the party and the whole collection was allocated to her. She also received about £400 from a fund subscribed by the citizens of Sydney. Baxter, on the intervention of the Governor, was at least offered a free passage to England, which he declined on the grounds that he would rather work his passage in order to make enough money to help the aged and paralysed lady he referred to as his "mother" (he was an orphan and she was in fact his grandmother, but had brought him up from childhood). He left for home on the barque *Elizabeth*; sailing in ballast she picked up a cargo of 6,355 bags of saltpetre, and 400 bags of Peruvian bark in South America. After an adventurous voyage she arrived at the London Docks on 24 June 1837, three days after Princess Victoria had been proclaimed Queen.

The convict Graham had meanwhile been ordered to Hyde Park, the prison headquarters in Sydney, where no doubt he was questioned by the colonial authorities with special reference to the nature of the country and inhabitants of the interior. He would have been in a position to meet, or to have been visited by, Mrs Fraser, but it is doubtful if she would have been anxious for a confrontation that would have brought back the painful past or to exchange social calls with a still undischarged convict. While

* A recent inspection of the files confirms Baxter's view that it never in fact appeared.

bureaucracy shuffled his papers Graham anxiously awaited news of his future. He had heard nothing by the New Year; from a petition (Appendix XI) written at that time drawing attention to his case, it may be deduced that he was frustrated and impatient. His laborious plea, containing frequent corrections and crossings out, increases the number of "canniballs" he had to contend with from four hundred to seven hundred. From the statement that he "by himself risqued all and freed all not as has been stated" it would seem that his earlier report to the Commandant at Moreton Bay had been questioned. He ended with a humble hope that "something may be done", a request that was in fact anticipated by a letter dated two days earlier (2 January 1837), in which an order from the Colonial Secretary's office finally resolved his future. He did not get his pardon but was given immediate freedom on a "ticket-of-leave", and a present worth at least £100 in today's currency.

"The Commandant of Moreton Bay having brought under notice the meritorious conduct of the Prisoner named in the margin (John Graham pr *Hooghly*) while employed in the expedition sent under the Command of Lieutenant Otter in search of the ship-wrecked crew of the Brig *Stirling Castle* I do my self the honour to inform you that Graham is to receive a Ticket of Leave and the sum of ten pounds to provide himself with the means of beginning, H.E. hopes, a new life and of hereafter maintaining himself by honest industry and I am directed by the Governor to request that you will prepare a Warrant for the issue of the above sum of ten pounds to Graham from the Military Chest."

The other convicts in the party were not forgotten, nor were they entirely forgiven—Walsh's life-sentence was reduced to seven years; the fourteen-year sentences of Williams, Paulgrove, Thompson and Phillips were halved, as were the seven-year sentences of Daley, King and Kinsella. Shannon, who had a spear through his thigh, and Brown, who had received only two years for "assault with intent to murder", also had a reduction of sentence."

XII

Variations On A Theme Of Rescue

Documents, official and unofficial, show beyond reasonable doubt that the convict Graham rescued Mrs Fraser and others from the *Stirling Castle* and fairly earned his reward and release. What subsequently became of him is not known; as there is no record of future convictions it might be assumed that he was able to "maintain himself by honest industry" as recommended by the Colonial Secretary. But objective fact in the *Stirling Castle* story is an elusive spirit and just as it is about to be grasped has the habit of changing its form. There is a theory, which has crystallised into local acceptance, that Graham's account of the rescue, for all its convincing circumstances, does not tell the whole story, and that Mrs Fraser's salvation involved another convict, living with the aborigines at the time, named Bracefell.

The Bracefell theory was fathered by Henry Stuart Russell, who tells the tale in his hodge-podge memoirs *Genesis of Queensland* (Turner & Henderson, 1888). Russell, a bluff upper-class Englishman, had arrived at Moreton Bay in the early part of 1842 just before the convict establishment was virtually disbanded and the territory officially declared open to settlement. Russell and a group of hearty "chums" seem to have arrived there in advance of anyone else and were already looking around for good sheep stations for themselves in the newly available grasslands. He and his companions—Andrew Petrie (whose family had come to Australia in an early voyage of the *Stirling Castle*), the Honourable Walter Wrottesley and a former midshipman called Jolliffe—planned an expedition to the northwards which would take them into the territory where the *Stirling Castle* drama had been enacted. Apart from looking for sheep "runs" they hoped to explore the then unmapped river* rumoured to debouch into the channel behind Great Sandy Island, and to look for the main ranges of the *bunya-bunya* pine, in which Petrie, its original discoverer, had a personal interest. They had also been asked to keep an eye open for two escaped convicts, known to have been living in the area for some years—David Bracefell and James Davies. They had been authorised by the last of the Commandants, Lieutenant Owen Gorman, to assure the escapees that they would not be punished if they gave themselves up.

They set off in a small boat with three "government men", as some categories of convict were known, to row. Having failed to reach the *bunya-bunya* forests owing to sandbanks in the area of the Maroochydore River, they pushed on to Noosa Head. Somewhere in this area Bracefell was known to be living with what Russell refers to as "Eumundy's tribe". Petrie had sent some aborigines they had met with a letter to the tribalised white man, and the party was waiting anxiously on the beach for some sort of response. In his typically breathless syntax Russell tells a strange and suspect story apparently convinced that it was true.

"But what had become of the blacks? They had managed to inform my friends that about two days' journey hence a white man had long been living with the neighbouring tribe; they themselves belonged to 'Eumundy's', a name known by report in Brisbane. This 'Eumundy' had the name of being a 'great fighting man', but was well-inclined towards the whites. Petrie had written a note—not under the impression that the runaway could read it, but as a token that his fellow men were at hand, promising these natives no end of 'bacca and blankets if they brought him to our camp. We had now been waiting two days, and the issue might soon be expected . . .

"In the afternoon of the third day two or three blacks were seen coming round the bay by the beach; by the glass we were

* The Mary River, so named after Governor Fitzroy's wife, who was killed in 1847 after her carriage horses bolted and dashed her against a tree.

able to make out that the one who carried the spear was not an aboriginal, though savage looking enough. Petrie and Wrottesley went to meet him, Joliffe and I took charge of the camp, in case of some demonstration, for, no doubt, there were plenty of the tribe hidden around us. The scene was curious. The poor fellow knew his own name—Bracefell—but could not recollect his own language for some time; had been quite unable to make out what Petrie's note meant, but heard enough to convince him that whites were at hand. At first (of course I now repeat his own story, which was told at odd times during our trip) he had felt overjoyed at the chance to open for his return to his fellow-men but, he declared, thoughts of the settlement filled him with terror. For a while he could not be persuaded that it was no longer the hell-on-earth which he had left years before, but tried to give every assurance that he would work 'his very best' if they would not flog him. He gradually became better-nerved by a general promise that he should not be in any way punished. In the past penal times the terrible 'cat' was mercilessly wielded over recovered runaways, in ready attendance upon heavy leg-irons day and night. He soon made himself useful in explaining to the blacks that we came with no hostile intent; had no wish in any way to molest them; and probably saved us much trouble in so doing in all earnestness. By the natives he was called 'Wandi', a 'great talker'; could speak the dialect of four different tribes (and it seemed that each tribe differed more or less in the manner of language and expression); would take his part in the fights, which seemed to be frequent, with their neighbours, but had never been persuaded to turn 'cannibal'. He was in looks an old man: his hard life had added its brand to the years of his seamed features. When washed and clothed, in a few days, he became perfectly naturalised; had recovered much confidence, and appeared to be really glad at having been rescued.

"This man had managed to escape from the chain to which he was manacled with others, not long after the arrival of Captain Logan as 'Commandant' of the penal settlement. He was living with 'Eumundy's' tribe, in which we had now found him, at the time of the wreck of the *Stirling Castle* on 'Great Sandy Cape'. The casting away of this ill-fated vessel was a signal for a general gathering of all the tribes within reach. Bracefell declared that they came in from hundreds and hundreds of miles all around, and had a grand 'tourr'. 'Eumundy', who was, I conclude, king of the tribe, was with his people at this rendezvous. The number assembled must have been unusually great. Captain Fraser, and some of the crew had been killed, for some cause, which was not explained; Brown, the mate, was reserved for future devilry. The Captain's wretched wife was spared, and had become 'domesticated'. It was the possession of this white woman, and the prospect of plunder, that had made these 'outsiders' so eager to reach the scene of the horror, and thus dare an invasion of a district on which, in fact, they knew they were trespassers. To open the ball, there was a general 'tourr', alias 'corroboree', in the good fellowship of common rejoicing.

"This 'Tourr', to which I afterwards walked with Bracefell at the back of 'Brown's Cape',* had been a ring scooped out of the soil in the fashion of a 'circus' of an immense size. The earth so collected formed a low mound which enclosed it all round the circumference, except at a point from which the path ran about a hundred yards into the thick underbrush, at the end of which —for it was a *cul de sac*—had stood the round low-roofed habitation of Mrs Fraser.

"Putting aside the torments of her bondage, Bracefell assured us that she was compelled to drag in wood for fires, and fetch water with as much cruelty as the 'gins' themselves. He was (Bracefell said) never allowed to speak to her, nor approach her. Her sufferings were terrible: he was always thinking of how she could manage to get away.

"Gathering from his yarn at odd times, that the first good

---

* Petrie named what is now Double Island Point "Brown's Cape" but, to his annoyance his place-names were never confirmed by the government. He also named Bracefell's Cape, which is officially Noosa Head.

fellowship quickly wore away; feuds sprung up: by waking up to jealousy of intrusion frequent fights came on, and off, in which some were killed and eaten, so tribe after tribe began to disappear or return to their own 'penates'. Eumundy was among the number who still lingered: he was so redoubtable a warrior that I think his presence was tolerated with discreet respect. Food had become scarce, and was becoming scarcer every day, too, where so many had assembled themselves. Under the pinch of empty stomachs the 'baggages' too would sneak away to forage for themselves: and so—it is quite intelligible—'Wandi', the great talker, found at length opportunities for interviewing poor Mrs Fraser. Her misery and want would soon have killed her; but the new-born hope of escape by this man's help brought back some courage. The occasion came. Food had come to famine prices, I concluded, when one by one they were forced to roam after honey, or scratching into ant-hills for the sweet little eggs; or tearing up grass-roots; or diving to the bottom of water holes for the bulbs of water-lilies, for a meal. Game—marsupial, but as keen-scented as our own Highland deer—had deserted the land; the *bunnia* was not bearing.

"Well, 'Where there's a will, there's a way', the will of the one helpless creature being nerved by her tremendous desolation; of the other by prospect of large reward, and that which under the despairing cry of the woman, had become 'father to his hope' —viz: the recovery of liberty by pardon, in return for this risky service to an Englishwoman.

"The way was found. She managed to escape the eye of the famishing creatures around on every side; met Bracefell at an appointed spot; with bent bodies waded along a running brook— here deep, here shallow; eyes and ears fright-quickened, hope-sustained; grasping every dear chance, by stone or stream, of passing over the treacherous ground without track or footfall, or fraying of grass or shrub, they reached a rugged range and hid themselves among the rocks.

"Bracefell turned to good purpose the native gifts bestowed by savagedom; fed his fellow fugitive on such bush diet as his wood-craft could compass, eluded the pursuit, and in a few days both set foot on a pathway well known to the hopeless, desperate runaway a few years ago.

"It is hard to accept the belief that under the reaction of supreme joy upon deliverance from such an agony of life as this woman's must have been, it could have been possible that any human soul should be possessed by any other power but that of unspeakable priceless gratitude to the worker out of such a restoration to kin and country.

"Yet I must accept it; nor I nor any friend of mine did, or did since, question the truth of Bracefell's story. Whether, as step by step she drew towards her asylum—with fears wakening, hope strengthening, dependence vanishing, faculties freshening—whether any doubt of her ability to honour her promises, fulfil her engagements, deliver her own soul by successful prayer for her outlawed benefactor's pardon and reward.

"Again, whether on approach to the paralysing scene of his unendurable helplessness, the entering within the brandish of the shrieking scourge—within the clutch on arm and ankle of the scalding iron—the riveting to the comrade chain—began to 'clam' the glimmer of his hope. The assurance sprung out of his voluntary service; partly, too, in compassion to a free, respectable British female citizen—whether the magnitude of such reward proportionally lessened his hope of getting it, or his protégée's ability—perhaps unwillingness—to make so grand an effort for such an end, and such an outcast—who can tell?

" 'What?' said he, 'as soon as we got on that path: as soon as she could see horse tracks, and trees cut down lying about, she knew she was at "Meginchen" (the natives' name for Brisbane). I told of all she said she would do when we got in, and told her I should like to hear all of it over again (with true cunning). She wouldn't speak; when she did as we went on she said she would complain of me.' "

" 'I turned round and ran back for my life!' Well do I even

now recollect the look of vindictive savagedom which accompanied this part of Bracefell's story. Speaking to him as I did day by day, watching for contradictions—not on this matter only —I became impressed with the persuasion that he had not made up a story like this, nor any other instance where I was seeking the truth. I believed him. In the episode just told, his excitement, manner, words, were too natural to be assumed for any concealment's sake—had there been anything to conceal.

"Under whatever impulse it was—he went back; seven years afterwards, or thereabouts, we found him with this tribe again.

" 'Were you not afraid to return after taking her away?' 'I was at first', answered Bracefell, when he had told me the sum of the above: 'not so much though, as I was of the settlement. After I got away there was a fight, too: but the woman didn't belong to us, so they didn't care about her bolting, and I've been with them ever since'."

If Russell had left it there, his story of Bracefell's dramatic involvement would have provided a more promising scource of speculation, but he seems to have become obsessed with a desire to prove his case and in so doing has destroyed much of its credibility. In the light of documents apparently not available to him, it can of course be demonstrated that his hypothesis is contradicted by the evidence. In addition it can be shown that he has gone beyond the bounds of honesty as well as credulity by "manipulating" certain extracts from the local newspapers of the period to support his case and establish that Mrs Fraser arrived at Moreton Bay independent of the Otter rescue party. Bracefell's story, as recounted by Russell, certainly has the ring of truth, but it is not improbable that he was telling something of a yarn to ingratiate himself with his rescuers—convicts were notorious for "acting up" or, as a witness before the Select Committee on Transportation (1838) phrased it, "they were excessively quick in what they call 'twigging a man'; that is, finding out his propensity, and immediately accommodating themselves to it." "Wandi", the "Great Talker", may have been better at the game than most.

Russell ruins his case by going on to say: "Mrs Fraser's escape by the help of a runaway convict, to Brisbane, was spoken of in my day. I heard no more of his disposal. Who was this Graham? Such a name never reached our ears . . . One record alone perhaps could settle the question, viz. Lieutenant Otter's own report of the event, if there be any in existence. If such is to be discovered, it must be in London.* And where's Lieutenant Otter? Poor Bracefell told the truth. Had he been caught when he brought in Mrs Fraser, we should not have found him, in 1842, where we did. It, doubtless, suited Mrs Fraser that she should be reported as one of the party rescued by Lieutenant Otter, under the guidance of 'Graham'."

Russell, compulsively developing the theory, goes on to suggest that Mrs Fraser had entered into some agreement with Bracefell, which she was unable or unwilling to fulfil, and in order to reconcile this story with the contradictory information that she had arrived with Otter's party, he attempts to rationalise it as follows: "The conclusion—to me at least—seems most reasonable, that the 'crew' met and brought in by the surveying party, had fallen in with each other during the course of their escape to the southward (Brisbane), consisted of the survivors, including Baxter; and about the same time Mrs Fraser had been, as said, guided to 'Meginchen' (the native name for Brisbane) by Bracefell —the sole witness to her degradation, and the sole being to whom she had placed herself under a heavy obligation which she dared not ignore while he was by her side, and might never be able to fulfil. Bracefell (when, in his expressive slang, she 'rounded upon him') left her in terror, and she was safe. Did she ever dream of his reappearing upon the stage in a new character? No! She became identified with those rescued by Lieutenant Otter."

Apart from an ambiguous reference in the diary of the expedition kept by Andrew Petrie, Russell's account is the prime source of the Bracewell story which, on the grounds of his perverted

* Lieutenant Otter's report is in fact to be found in the archives held by the Mitchell Library in Sydney. (Appendix X.)

evidence, might reasonably be discounted. Yet the version has interesting aspects which cannot be entirely ignored. Bracefell was indeed in the Wide Bay area at the time and might well have met Mrs Fraser and, if not, would certainly have been aware of her presence, though, as an escaped convict, wary of agents from the outside world, he might have preferred to keep out of her way. Assuming they did meet, could she herself have had some reason for keeping their association secret? It might be thought that the Commandant, with an ear to the "intelligence" of the settlement through his overseers and constables, and being further in a position to cross-question the protagonists, would somehow have heard if another convict had been involved. But recapitulating the affair twenty years later, when there could be no further need for discretion or security, Fyans describes Graham making contact with Mrs Fraser in a tantalisingly unrevealing passage. "Graham saw Mrs Fraser, endeavoured to speak with her, which she avoided, saying that the white men she had met were worse than the blacks. Here, he said to her, read this paper. She did so, getting into an argument inquiring who it was written by. The commandant. Who is he? Time was precious to Graham, who urged her, explaining during the Corroboree we shall leave. About twelve o'clock Graham had his prize . . ."

There is mystery in the air. Who were the hateful "white men", one of whom she seems to have at first taken her rescuer to be? She must surely have been referring to escaped convicts living in the bush. Had she been molested by all or any of them? They might well have turned up at the *corroboree* grounds—Bracefell, "Tallboy" Banks, "Tursi", Samuel Derrington, "Durrambhoi" Davies, all of whom were at large in the area at that time, and it is tempting to speculate on their crude familiarities, individual or collective.

Though there is no positive reference to such an encounter other than Russell's story, it is conceivable that she had in fact formed some relationship with Bracefell involving a secret shame she wished to keep concealed. It is not impossible that he may even have brought her to the outskirts of Moreton Bay as he claimed, before a quarrel had caused him to abandon her to recapture by the blacks. A less fanciful supposition is that Graham was helped by Bracefell in the rescue operation. Was he, indeed, the person described in Graham's original narrative as "a man by the name of Mothervane", who claimed Mrs Fraser as his wife's sister and therefore his possession? It is an interesting fact that the word for "ghost" in the Kabi dialect is *mŏth'ar* and *derwhain* (emu) was a common local name-group to which Bracefell might have been attached. As Mŏth'ar Derwhain or "Mothervane", Bracefell might have made unwelcome overtures to Mrs Fraser and indeed claimed her as his wife and used her as such. Should she have at first encouraged him, perhaps with the intention of using him to help her in escape, she may have decided to say nothing about it later for fear of compromising herself. Graham and Bracefell, as one convict to another, may have come to terms and formulated a rescue plan that involved an apparent quarrel over their rights to Mrs Fraser; she may have promised Bracefell that if the plan was successful she would intercede for him should he wish to return to Moreton Bay. Perhaps he was one of the "four natives" who accompanied Graham and Mrs Fraser to the rendezvous with Otter, and it is then that some such conversation as Russell reported actually took place. Mrs Fraser, remembering his earlier conduct, may have threatened to denounce him to the hated military he could actually see on the beach below. Graham, with a sense of loyalty towards a fellow convict in distress, and anxious not to share the glory or detract in the least degree from his claim to remission and reward, may have sworn Mrs Fraser to secrecy, which, in any case, she would be anxious to maintain in protection of her own reputation.

In fact, the records show that Bracefell was betrayed by Derrington* a year later and brought back to Moreton Bay. He

---

* Samuel Derrington absconded from Moreton Bay five months after Graham. He gave himself up on October 17, 1836, not long after Mrs Fraser had left for Sydney. He claimed to have helped some of the *Stirling*

was flogged and absconded again, where he remained until Russell brought him out. Unlike the case of Derrington, there is no record of Bracefell telling the prison authorities the story of his aid to Mrs Fraser, which might have been expected to improve his position. Perhaps he told it hopefully, was disbelieved, and returned in chagrin to his more reliable aboriginal friends.

There is another ingredient in the mysterious rescue. Mrs Fraser's English biographer, John Curtis, who frequently interviewed her, introduces a brawny black called Gormandy (presumably the Eumundy referred to by Russell, and possibly the "Bully" in Graham's report), who picks her up by the waist and carries her to safety in the best romantic tradition, a variation that may have been embroidered by Curtis with the intention of enhancing the value of his "serial rights". Before giving the Curtis account of the rescue it is interesting to read the American or "nick-of-time" version as it continues after the previous instalment. It will be recalled that Mrs Fraser is about to be raped by

---

Castle party and wanted remission for it. But apparently Foster Fyans did not believe his story as he was sentenced to serve out his full term of 14 years.

In May 1837 he acted as guide to Lieutenant Otter in an expedition to investigate reports of another shipwreck in the Wide Bay area. In his report on the affair Otter wrote:

"The next day (16 May) the natives came in and we ascertained beyond doubt that the story of a vessel being wrecked was totally false. I therefore determined to make the best of my way back to the Settlement. Hearing, however, that a runaway of the name of Bracefield (sic.) who had been out for six or seven years, was in the neighbourhood, I remained for a day for the purpose of apprehending him, in which I succeeded with the aid of Derrington who persuaded the blacks to assist us."

Bracewell was to abscond again almost immediately, and remained in the bush until brought in by the Russell expedition. He was pardoned on April 24, 1839.

Bracewell was to lead the Russell expedition to another bushranger, at large in the area of the Mary River—James Davies, from Glasgow, whose native name was "Durrambhoi". Davies at first thought Bracewell had betrayed him, but was glad to return with the expedition when he learned about the new state of affairs at Moreton Bay.

an aged chief who, "fiend-like", has forced her into his "dismal and filthy cabin". Now read on:

"As a most remarkable instance of the interposition of Divine Providence, they arrived in season to frustrate the designs of the savage brute, who had selected me as his victim, and to rescue me from one of the most alarming situations in which an unfortunate female could be placed! I at that instant was held fast by the savage a few paces from the hut, and was first discovered by Mr Graham, who was a short distance ahead of the others, and was attracted to the thicket by my moans and entreaties for mercy! The first knowledge that I had of his approach was by the sudden flight of the savage by whom I had been seized and held with an iron grasp, and by whom Mr G. was first discovered. He made no attempt to intercept the affrighted savage, but caught me in his arms, and hurried me to the boat, in which we all immediately embarked, before the savage islanders had time to collect in sufficient numbers to oppose us."

Was the "savage brute", who seems from his gallant proposal quoted in an earlier chapter to have spoken English, none other than "Mothervane" Bracefell acting out the rescue plot? Her violator is described as "aged", whereas Bracefell would then be under forty. Russell, however, on seeing him for the first time, described him as "in looks an old man".

In the rescue story that follows, which, according to Curtis, Mrs Fraser learned from Graham, it is strange that so contradictory a report should have gone unchallenged by the authorities at Moreton Bay, in this case Foster Fyans and his lieutenant, Otter, who, from his letter to his sister, appears to have known of a third party, "a kind of chief". A possible explanation is that Fyans, having on his own initiative promised Graham a pardon if he was successful, had exceeded his authority and, needing confirmation from his superiors in Sydney, had been in collusion with Graham in the production of the report on which his bid for manumission depended. It seems unlikely that Mrs Fraser, even in her demented state, had imagined her abduction by the giant Gormandy, who was presumably "Eumundy", the local strong man. Perhaps she had dealings with him on another occasion. In any event she makes no mention of him in her first official statement taken down by the authorities at Moreton Bay shortly after her return. She simply says: "a white man whose name I have since heard is Graham came up and told me he had been sent for me, and that there was succour at hand—he spoke to the natives for some time and after a good deal of altercation succeeded in getting me away."

The Curtis version of her rescue runs as follows:

"It appears by the statement made to her by Graham, that he fell in with a native with whom he had been acquainted during the time he was a fugitive in the bush, and to whom he gave the soubriquet of Gormondy, owing to his being a most inveterate gormandizer. This fellow was an amazingly powerful man, and few of his tribe cared much to offend him. Although he did not stand in the character of a chief with them, yet he formed a useful adjunct to their party, as he was a mighty man of war as well as a mighty eater. Having made this man his friend, he confided to him the nature of his mission to a certain extent, by representing that he was in quest of a white female who was related to him, and as she was ill-treated by the tribe she was with, he told Gormondy if he would rescue her, he (Graham) would reward him with mocoes, tomahawks and other instruments; and as an additional inducement, he was told that if he got her away and she should be loth to leave the bush, the female should become his exclusive companion. Thus encouraged, he undertook to work her deliverance. After this preliminary was settled, Graham was ordered to proceed to a place where he had appointed to meet with Gormondy, and he started a long time before Lieutenant Otter and his soldiers followed in the boat, it having been previously arranged that the harbinger should make a particular mark on the sandy beach where the boat was to halt. On its arrival, he was to proceed with Gormondy from the hiding place, in order to carry their scheme into effect if possible; and should it be necessary, he was to fire a pistol or blow a trumpet, with which he was provided, and then the soldiers were to proceed in the direction of the sound. In order to avoid suspicion, Gormondy was to appear hostile to Graham for a time, the latter on this occasion being well dressed, in order to excite their cupidity, and they soon divested him of his clothing. He had also provided himself with trinkets of various kinds, as well as some clippings of tin, of which they are very fond, and use as ornaments for the head; these he distributed to them voluntarily, and intimated that he could get them a quantity more of the same articles. It was then proposed that they should have a corrobery on the occasion, which was agreed to. It had been planned between Graham and Gormondy that during the dance the former was to go down a vista which led to the water-side and this he did without exciting any suspicion in the minds of the natives. The latter was then to watch his opportunity and run off with Mrs Fraser, to whom it had been made known by her deliverer, that a plan had been laid for her rescue, and that she was to be placed in a canoe if possible, and cross the lake to an island where an officer and file of men lay in ambush.

"The unfortunate lady could not describe to us the sensations with which her mind was affected at this period—hopes and fears alternately arose, but the latter she says preponderated. She was enabled, however, at some intervals, to trust in God, and hope for a release; but as to the manner in which it was to be effected, she was partly ignorant, especially as Graham had suddenly withdrawn from the company. (Mrs Fraser states, that notwithstanding the presents Graham made to the natives, they cried *woobra*, *woobra* (an expression of anger), spat in his face, and poured upon him every contumely, which called for the interference of Gormondy, who assured the tribe that through him (Graham) they would receive a further present. At a period of the dance, when the attention of the party is more excited than at others, Gormondy motioned her to be silent; he then ran up to the spot where she was standing, and embracing her round the middle with his gigantic arms, he swung her on his back, and ran like lightning between the trees to the beach, where Graham was waiting for them with a canoe, into which she was placed, and the little bark swiftly glided across the smooth surface of the lake, to the middle of which they had arrived before the natives had discovered their absence; and they not having their canoes on that part of that shore, some time elapsed before pursuit could be made. Before she joined Lieutenant Otter, however, three or four of the tribe overtook them, and appeared very unwilling to give her up. Graham told them they would be handsomely rewarded with mocoes and other articles. He then made a signal, and Lieutenant Otter sent her a cloak and petticoat to put on, to prevent her appearing in a state of nudity before the boat's crew and soldiers. At this time she was very much fatigued, owing to the long walk she had the day before, and the joy which she felt, appeared rather to increase than allay her exhaustion. She says, that she felt almost spellbound; the work of the last hour seemed to her to be so mysterious that she could scarcely believe it a reality."

"Gormondy" seems to have been no fiction; it might have added an interesting twist to the plot if David Bracefell could have been that "amazingly powerful man". But alas! the records show that he was only 5 ft 4 ins and could thus hardly have "embraced her round the middle with his gigantic arms".

There had evidently been some questions asked in official quarters as to the precise part Graham played in the rescue, resulting perhaps from his own, Derrington's, or Mrs Fraser's misrepresentations. In his last petition for release, written from Hyde Park, he had protested impatiently that he "thus by himself risqued all and freed all not as has been stated". Until other evidence turns up let John Graham have the last word and the benefit of the doubt.

As for Mrs Fraser, Russell referred to her in an uncompromisingly hostile tone: "Her imposition upon the Londoners, which I shrink from explaining but recollect well, tallied well with my today conjectures as to her character. The 'issue' of the general sympathy is 'pillowed' on my recollection of laughable frauds successfully practised at that time in London."

The story Russell "shrank from explaining" is told in the following chapters.

XIII

Mrs Fraser's New Captain

Mrs Fraser was leisurely recuperating, seemingly not over-anxious to return to her responsibilities in the Orkneys, when a brig about the same size as the *Stirling Castle* put into Sydney Harbour from New Zealand. She was the *Mediterranean Packet*, commanded by Captain Alexander John Greene. In the course of a recent trading expedition to New Zealand he had been involved in a minor skirmish aboard his ship when one of his crew had killed a native for stealing an axe. A Maori chief had sworn to kill the captain in revenge and Greene, hearing of the plot, had sensibly moved his ship from the area. This event was mis-reported at length in the Sydney papers and no doubt he and Mrs Fraser were introduced at some local gathering as having common ground for conversation.

Had they in fact met before, perhaps in some other port of call? Was Captain Greene an old shipmate of Captain Fraser and had he cast interested glances in the direction of his friend's wife before her unfortunate experience? Or did he see her as an agreeable widow with a publicly subscribed "nest-egg" equal to three years at sea at the going rate of pay for captains of smaller vessels? There is no information at present available on these matters, but one thing is known for certain—the records of New South Wales show that on February 23rd 1837 at the Presbyterian Church of St Andrew, "Eliza Anne Slack or Fraser, widow, and Alexander John Greene, Master Mariner" were "joined together in wedlock" by the Reverend John McGarvie. Witnesses were Andrew Lang, Elizabeth Edwards (who signed with a cross), Henry Carmichael and James Edwards. None of these names are those of known friends in Sydney, so it is likely that, wishing to keep the marriage a secret, they collected a few people from a different social stratum. The public wedding of a widow so recently bereaved would at that date have been considered nothing less than a scandal.

Two days after the wedding the *Mediterranean Packet* set sail for England. The passenger list read: Mr Small, Mrs Frazier (sic), Mr and Mrs Edwards (perhaps the witnesses at the wedding), Joseph and John Beatley, John Wilson, W. Clary, R. Lenox, John Kelly and Lucy Chapman. Her unromantic cargo was 27 casks of black oil, 45 tons of whalebone, 3,000 treenails, 27 casks of red and white lead, and 215 bales of wool.

The *Mediterranean Packet* arrived at Liverpool, Britain's second largest seaport with even more public houses per head of population than Sydney, on July 16th 1837. There are some tantalising glimpses of Mrs Fraser (Greene) in that city—at church, soliciting at the Parish Office, promenading the streets in her finery—insubstantial manifestations emanating from the office of the Commissioner for Police, but embedded in a compromising indictment. On her first arrival she had applied to Mr Dowling, the Commissioner, for money to go to London where she said she had friends who would contribute to her support. "At the date of her application", the report says, "she was very indifferently attired, her clothes being, as she said, procured from the parties in Sydney to whom she was indebted for the kindness she experienced after her return thither from among the savages. Mr Dowling, satisfied that she was in the distress that she represented, acquainted the Mayor and parochial authorities of Liverpool with her case and arrangements were made for affording her the assistance she solicited. According to appointment she called at the Parish Office in Fenwick Street, and again recapitulated the details of her shipwreck in the *Stirling Castle* and subsequent privations and sufferings. In reply to some questions put to her respecting the savages with whom she professed to have been so long domiciled, she detailed few particulars, compared with

which the marvels witnessed by the renowned Mr Lemuel
Gulliver would be very common-place matters indeed. Among
other singularities she said that the barbarians had large tufts of
blue hair growing upon their shoulders in the form of epaulets,
and that their heads were quite denuded of hair, with the exception of the crown of the head from which streamed a large portion
of the same texture and colour as the material forming their
shoulder ornaments.

"Mr Dowling's confidence in her veracity immediately under-
went a considerable diminution, and ordering her contemplated
relief to be suspended for some time, he sent for the captain of the
vessel in which she arrived from Sydney. The captain being
absent on business the mate came in his stead, and evinced considerable reluctance to give any information relative to the person
calling herself Mrs Fraser. After a good deal of hesitation, however, he admitted that she was in no distress whatever; that she
had an abundance of clothes of a very superior description; and
moreover that she was married to the captain, whose name was
Greene, and consequently could want for nothing any woman in
her sphere of life had a right to expect. Upon being taxed with
her imposition in representing herself destitute and avoiding all
mention of her marriage to Greene, she said that he had treated
her with great harshness, and she was desirous of separating from
him and going to London. Mr Dowling then procured the
attendance of Greene himself, who did not deny the fact of his
being married to her and consented to supply her with the
necessary means of prosecuting her journey to the metropolis.
Some time after they were seen repeatedly in Liverpool, promenading the principal streets, and at church, she being dressed
very showily, with a white veil, bracelets and other indications of
a well-stocked wardrobe. Nothing further transpired in Liverpool
respecting her, and the police authorities then regarded her
statement merely in the light of an attempted fraud, of which
numerous instances are perpetually falling within their cogniz-
ance."

What were the Greenes up to? Was Captain Greene a sort of Svengali exploiting his wife's susceptibility and, as might appear from her rambling remarks about bald-headed, blue-epauletted savages, mental confusion or madness? Had he taken charge of her money? Did she really want to get away from him to London, or were they co-plotters from the start? Certainly they went to London together, where financial assistance was most likely to be found, and his manipulation of her affairs is in evidence there. Mrs Fraser had been advised by the authorities in Sydney to apply to the Colonial Office for assistance and was provided with documents in that name vouching for her as a widow in needy circumstances who had undergone most harrowing experiences. On August 17th, still calling herself Mrs Fraser, she presented herself at Whitehall and applied for an interview with the Secretary of State for the Colonies, Lord Glenelg. There was no question of a lady of her limited social connection confronting so august a personage—she was asked to leave her particulars, which she did in the form of an equivocal petition written by Captain Greene:

Sir,

Having accompanied the widow of the late Capt. Fraser (who was wrecked on the East Coast of New Holland, while on their passage from Sydney to Singapore via Torres Straits) to this office, I beg therefore to submit to your Lordship's notice that the said widow after having remained for some months among the savages was rescued therefrom by the indefatigable exertions of the Commandant at Moreton Bay, and subsequently conveyed therefrom to Sydney by his Excellency's command on board of the Revenue Cutter sent thither expressly for this purpose. During the said widow's stay at Sydney very little was done for her in a pecuniary point of view, further than enabling her to purchase a few articles of clothing, paying this for her passage and purchasing the necessaries for her subsistence during the passage. The said widow having at length arrived destitute of money, and almost so in apparel, having a family in Scotland unprovided for, I therefore on her behalf beg to convey to your Lordship the circumstances in which she is now placed.

I remain your Lordship's humble servant,
John Greene.

Returning a few days later, as instructed, for an answer, she was told that her case "had not passed a thorough review". When she next called she learned that the Colonial Secretary had left word, in the best manner of Dickens's Office of Circumlocution, that "if he saw any reason he would communicate with her". In the official jargon of the day this was as much as to say "your petition is dismissed".*

Helpful friends then advised her to call on the Reverend George Smith,† the redoubtable founder and incumbent of the Mariners' Church, Wellclose Square in the neighbourhood of the Docks. The Reverend Smith was known as "Boatswain" Smith on account of his former service in the navy and dedicated interest in the welfare of seamen and their distressed dependants; a benevolent but eccentric character, who signed himself in parenthesis B.B.U. (Burning Bush Unconsumed), he was then away on one of his regular fund-raising trips, touring the country with twelve orphan boys dressed as soldiers and sailors to sing patriotic songs and hymns. But his second-in-command listened to the story with sympathy and advised her to go to the Mansion House and see if the Lord Mayor of London could help. On his return

* Captain Greene's petition, filed in the Public Records Office, is minuted: "Answer that there are no funds at Lord G's disposal applicable to the relief of Mrs Fraser."

† George Charles Smith (1782–1863) had joined the navy involuntarily— apprenticed to the master of a U.S. brig he had been press-ganged into the British navy while at Surinam. He fought at the Battle of Copenhagen, leaving the navy in 1803. He became a Baptist minister and concerned himself with the welfare of seamen. He wrote a book called "Intemperance, or a General View of the Abundance, the Influence and the Horrible Consequences of Ardent Spirits". At the age of eighty he visited the United States and preached in New York, Boston and Salem. He died in poverty in Penzance, where over 2,000 people attended his funeral.

"Boatswain" Smith interested himself further in her case, taking a collection and preaching a sermon for her in his church, and composing a moving poem dedicated to her drowned baby (Appendix XII).

The Lord Mayor of London, Thomas Kelly, who was also Chief Magistrate, was more sympathetic than the Colonial Secretary and agreed to set up a committee to enquire into her circumstances and, if deserving, to launch a public subscription. The first session, held in the Justice Room on August 23rd, was attended by journalists and reported the following day in the national press. Representing *The Times* was John Curtis, her subsequent biographer, who had previously covered the famous "Murder in the Red Barn" story and written it up into a book. Curtis had invented a system of shorthand on which he had published a treatise,* and so was better equipped than most to take things down. But on this occasion he had some difficulty, prefacing his report with the disclaimer: "The following is as close an account as our reporter could collect from a statement necessarily confused and incoherent".

Her story as reported in *The Times* holds to the main facts outlined in this narrative, with the exception of a strange tale of the death of James Major, who, from more reliable sources, we know died under different circumstances somewhere between Moreton Bay and Sydney. Although copied by Curtis, this sinister little story has not been reported elsewhere except in "Mournful Verses" quoted as an introduction, nor was it recounted by any member of the crew. It is likely to have been a fantasy of her confused mind, a nightmare dredged up from travellers' tales told by her husband.

This was the version printed in *The Times*:

"Two days after this horrible event [the death of Brown] a fine-looking young man named James Major was disposed of. Captain Fraser, who knew a good deal of the character and habits

* "Shorthand made Shorter, or Stenography Simplified, being a Concise Introduction to a Complete Knowledge of the Art", London, 1835.

of the savages on this coast, had mentioned to Major that the savages would take off his head for a figure bust for one of their canoes. It seemed, too, that it was usual for the savage who contemplated that sort of execution to smile in the face of his victim immediately before he struck him to the earth. While Major was at work, the chief of the tribe approached him and tapped him on the shoulder. At this instant the poor fellow received a blow on the back of the neck from a waddie or crooked stick, which stunned him. He fell to the ground, and a couple of savages set to work, and by means of sharpened shells severed the head from the body with frightful lacerations. They then ate parts of the body, and preserved the head with certain gums of extraordinary efficacy and affixed it as a figure bust to one of their canoes."

This incident is all the more unlikely because the Australian aborigines were not known to treat heads in such a manner, nor were their simple bark canoes equipped with an appropriate prow to which a human head might advantageously be attached. One can hear the Captain spinning a yarn aboard ship, to which his wife had listened disapprovingly, basing his ideas on the head-preserving habits of the New Zealand natives—though forbidden by government edict,* a discreditable business in Sydney at that

* "Whereas it has been represented to his Excellency the Governor, that the masters and crews of vessels trading between this Colony and New Zealand, are in the practice of purchasing and bringing from thence human heads, which are preserved in a manner peculiar to that country; And whereas there is strong reason to believe, that such disgusting traffic tends greatly to increase the sacrifice of human life among savages whose disregard of it is notorious, his Excellency is desirous to check it by all the means in his power, and with this in view, his Excellency has been pleased to order, that the Officers of the Customs do strictly watch and report every instance which they may discover of an attempt to import into the Colony any dried or preserved human heads in future, with the names of all parties concerned in every such attempt.

"His Excellency trusts that to put a total stop to this traffic, it is necessary for him only thus to point out the almost certain and dreadful consequences which may be expected to ensue from a continuance of it, and the scandal and prejudice which it cannot fail to raise against the name and character

time was the sale of tattooed Maori heads, known in the trade as
"Baked Heads". Prices in the shops ranged from one to two
guineas according to the amount of tattooing, but cheaper ones,
smuggled in by seamen, were hawked around the port.

Though there was no mention of savages with blue hair on
their shoulders this time, Mrs Fraser told another dubious story
in her evidence:

"They were always at war with the other tribes, and they began
to teach me the way to use the spear and shield. The black woman
I followed also brought me with her to lie in wait for snakes,
which frequently formed our meals. Mrs — has the skin of a
large snake I helped to kill, and by which I thought I should have
been killed, for it coiled round me like a boa constrictor, but the
black woman smashed its head with a waddie." Mrs Fraser might
indeed have had encounters with constrictors in the rain forests,
but her story is not supported by any mention in Australia, where
the sight of her carrying a skin after her rescue and subsequently
presenting it to a local lady is hardly likely to have gone un-
reported. But there was no doubt about the sincerity of her
summing up:

"The stories which we have read in our childhood, and the
representations we have seen in the theatres of savage life are
mere trifles compared with the real facts. When first I heard their
frightful yell, I expected nothing but destruction; but I never

---

of British Traders, in a country with which it is now become highly important
for the merchants and traders of this Colony, at least, to cultivate feelings
of natural goodwill; but if his Excellency should be disappointed in this
reasonable expectation, he will feel it an imperative duty to take strong
measures for totally suppressing the inhuman and very mischievous traffic
in question.

"His Excellency further trusts, that all persons who have in their possession
human heads, recently brought from New Zealand and particularly by the
schooner *Prince of Denmark* will immediately deliver them up for the purpose
of being restored to the relatives of the deceased parties to whom these
heads belonged; this being the only possible reparation that can be rendered,
and application having been specially made to his Excellency to the purpose."

expected to witness anything like what I have seen. There is no difference between these savages and the beasts of the forest, except that the savages are ingenious in their cruelty. All that the race of man can conceive falls short of what I have witnessed."

After her rambling statement had concluded, the Lord Mayor asked her about her financial circumstances. Captain Greene, who had accompanied her to the hearing, urgently volunteered that "the unfortunate lady is not mistress of a farthing". The clothes on her back, he said, had been given her by the Commandant's wife at Moreton Bay, and Captain Fraser had been the sole support of her three young children, who were in the Orkney Islands, to which she was anxious to return as soon as possible. Captain Greene added, almost as if an insurance claim were at issue, that "she was lame and had also lost the use of one arm and the sight of one eye by the severity of the inflictions to which she had been subjected".

The Lord Mayor was apparently impressed and moved by the testimony and said that he "had never heard anything so truly dreadful in all his experience". He added that he was sure that "the ladies of London, who were constantly looking for such objects, would speedily relieve her", and that he would willingly receive contributions for her benefit. Mrs Fraser (Greene) was later introduced to the Lady Mayoress, who to some extent lessened the effect of the drama by saying, and her possibly ironic observation was quoted in the press, that she "was not a little surprised at the healthy and placid appearance of a woman who had been doomed to a companionship compared with which an intercourse with the beasts of the wilderness would have been a refuge and a consolation."

Attending the court was John Baxter, who had been sought out by the Greenes in his Commercial Road lodgings on their arrival in London. Called the following day to give evidence, he confirmed Mrs Fraser's general account, though he made no mention of the slaying of James Major. He horrified the Lord

Mayor with his story about "drawing lots" as to who should be the first to be eaten in the long-boat, and his description of how he had been offered parts of a human baby to eat while living with the aborigines. The Lord Mayor commented: "Anything so fearful I never heard since I was born."

XIV

Darge's Testimony

The following day, waiting for news in a Mansion House ante-room, the Greenes and Baxter were surprised by the entry of a familiar figure. It was "Big Bob" Darge who, having read reports of the inquiry in the papers, had presented himself in the hope, perhaps, of a share of the pickings. The Lord Mayor set himself to question this "independent witness" and their ensuing dialogue presented a more understanding assessment of aboriginal attitudes:

The Lord Mayor : You have seen the extraordinary accounts which have been published in the newspapers, and are one of the men who were cast away amongst the savages?

Darge : I have seen the statements, and but for them I should not have known any comrade of mine was in London.

The Lord Mayor : Did you frequently see Mrs Fraser after the natives separated the crew from each other?

Darge : Never but once, until she was brought into Moreton Bay by Lieutenant Otter's detachment. I escaped some days before, along with Joseph Corralis, the steward, and Youlden, another of the seamen. There is a mistake as to Graham the convict saving me. I got away without his assistance or knowledge, and I and Joseph Corralis were the first that gave information to Lieutenant Otter of the condition of the crew, before the bushranger was employed to get them away.

The Lord Mayor : You was along with a separate tribe, and was, I suppose, the slave of the tribe?

Darge : I was obliged to accompany a different tribe, but I was often changed from one tribe to another, and I was sent about to cut down and carry trees to light fires, and carry water.

The Lord Mayor: What sort of treatment did you experience?

Darge: Very hard. I was worked till I was reduced to a skeleton, and I don't suppose I shall ever quite recover the injuries I have endured in my constitution. We had sharp nights and very heavy dews and rains, and I was exposed naked to everything.

The Lord Mayor: The natives would not allow you to wear anything?

Darge: Nothing. They would not even permit me to put a leaf or a piece of bark upon any part of my body. They seemed to hate all covering on others as well as themselves.

The Lord Mayor: And they made no distinction between males and females in that respect?

Darge: Not the least, except with unmarried women. Before their women had husbands they wore a piece of bark round their waists; but from the moment they became wives, they cast away the covering and stood just as they were born.

The Lord Mayor: Did there appear to be any jealousy amongst them?

Darge: I did not perceive it; but some ran away with the wives of those of other tribes sometimes, but it was the winter of that part of the world when we were with the natives, and they had a great deal to do very often to manage to live.

The Lord Mayor: To live appeared to be all their care?

Darge: It was, and we had to work severely to get fish and kangaroos. We generally had enough of *bungwa*, which is a kind of root of fern growing in swampy ground. It is like our mountain fern, and tasted deliciously to me, but we were obliged to eat a kind of purgative grass to prevent its bad effects upon our constitution.

The Lord Mayor: Did they seem to delight in annoying you?

Darge: Not the men who were grown up. The young people from 10 to 14 or 15 years old, used to annoy me deliberately with goads and fire-sticks. I was unable to sit cross-legged like a tailor, as they used to sit, and they could not bear to see that, so they used to torment me. When they sat down, they looked like a nation of black tailors; but I cannot call them a cruel people.

The Lord Mayor: You do not think, although the natives killed others of the crew, that they had any intention to kill you?

Darge: I don't think they would have killed me. But there were some who could not bear the sight of a white man at all. I believe that the reason they had such a hatred of me was that the soldiers wounded them. I observed in particular that a man who lost his leg had a desperate hatred of me, and he tried to kill me three or four times.

The Lord Mayor: You believe he was injured by the soldiers?

Darge: I have no doubt of it. There is intercourse between some of the tribes and the military, and these tribes used to betray the bushrangers to the soldiers for a *moco* or axe. When a bushranger that the Government wished to get back ran away from labour amongst the distant tribes, the soldiers were sure to employ some of the less barbarous tribes to restore him, and they rewarded the natives with an axe or *moco*, or a fishing hook which they call a *gilla gilla*. For either of these instruments I am sure they would kill their fathers and mothers.

The Lord Mayor: Did they seem attached to their wives?

Darge: Not at all. They seem to care nothing about them, but they are very fond of their children. They beat their wives dreadfully.

The Lord Mayor: Have you reason to believe that they are cannibals?

Darge: I do not believe that any of the tribes I was amongst ate human flesh. I never saw anything of the kind. They used not to hand anything to me to eat; they used to throw it. When they were done with their fish-bones they used to throw them to me, and as often as the young natives could they prevented me from getting any. Their dogs too, had a great aversion to white men, and used to howl at me.

The Lord Mayor: The natives obliged Mrs Fraser and Baxter to make themselves as like as possible to them. Was that the case with respect to you?

Darge: They put cockatoo feathers at each side of my head, and stuck small feathers of the most beautiful birds all over it, and they sometimes drew red streaks across my eyebrows, sometimes they rubbed my cheeks with red stuff, and they used to do so with themselves. They put me to a great deal of pain in plucking out my beard and whiskers, which they could not bear. They plucked out their own always; and after they pulled me about and daubed me all over, they would point to me to look in the water at myself. Although we could see ourselves in the stream, they used to take up water in a sort of bucket made of the bark of trees to see their faces in and they made me do the same.

The Lord Mayor: Did they oblige you to catch fish for them?

Darge: No, I had the most laborious employment. They used to fish themselves, and they had great skill in fishing. They used to spear, and could strike a fish at a great distance; and they sometimes used a net, with which they used to go in a crowd into shallow water and surround a fish. This net they spun across their knees with bark they call *corrigin*.

The Lord Mayor: Were they naked?

Darge: As when they were born.

The Lord Mayor: You say that you and Corralis, the black steward, were together for a considerable time? How did they treat him?

Darge: They treated him well, but he dared not to throw me anything in their presence. If he had a bit of fish to spare he was afraid to throw it to me.

The Lord Mayor: How then did you contrive to get away?

Darge: Joseph Corralis and Youlden, who was very ill, and I, got away towards the water along with one of the natives, to whom we promised a *moco* and a *gilla gilla*, to show us the way to the place inhabited by the colonists. As we went along we

were obliged to leave Youlden in the bush, as he was unable
to walk, and we were unable to carry him. After going along
the beach for some time we saw a boat, but we thought it
belonged to a bushranger. We, however, soon heard two shots,
and then we were sure that we were near relief, and in a very
short time, while our hearts were leaping within us, we saw a
soldier make his appearance.

The Lord Mayor: The detachment, I suppose, who were in search
of you?

Darge: Not at all. Nothing was known about us at this time at
Moreton Bay. We found it was Lieutenant Otter, who had
come on a pleasure party, and he was astonished to find that
we were wrecked seamen. The coxswain of his boat went up
with the native who accompanied us to the place where Youlden
lay, and brought him up next day, and Lieutenant Otter conveyed us all to Moreton Bay, and then employed Graham, the
convict, to go in search of the rest of the crew.

The Lord Mayor: Then you were in communication with Graham?

Darge: Yes, certainly; he was perfectly well acquainted with the
natives. When we spoke of particular places he knew everything about them, and described them to us, and he seemed
to know where the rest of the crew were to be found.

The Lord Mayor: Did you see Mrs Fraser upon her appearance
at Moreton Bay?

Darge: I was present when she came into the place, and helped
to carry her.

The Lord Mayor: There was evidently a difference between the
tribes?

Darge: Some had curly hair, and some long straight hair, and
some were copper colour. Those with whom I was were the
coarsest of human beings, the most savage possible. They can't
bear the idea of covering, and they make themselves even more
hideous than they are. They not only daub their faces and
bodies frightfully, but they bore a hole through the flesh between the nostrils, and poke into it a piece of kangaroo-fur.

The Lord Mayor: The native who acted as your guide was of course rewarded?

Darge: He received a *moco*, and some of the natives brought Youlden in on their shoulders, thinking that they would get a *moco* amongst them, but I do not know whether they got anything. The Government keep these things in readiness to present them with in case they should want to send after any desperate bushranger that might happen to escape from punishment; and the punishment is now so great in the settlement that the convicts are glad to get away from it.

The Lord Mayor: The convicts in this country have been long in the habit of considering that transportation was merely a removal from one country to another. The commutation of the penalty of death, however, to that of transportation is, it appears, no very great gain to the unfortunate criminal when he preferred the horrible alternative of a communion with savages. Did the females appear to approach nearer to ordinary humanity than the men?

Darge: No. They are not so strong, that's all. They worried me, and indeed all of us desperately, till they took every stitch from our persons. The statement that we were stripped of our clothes at once is wrong. We were for some time on the beach before we lost all our clothes. The natives were first very shy, and used to come round us and steal our things; they tempted us with fire to warm us, and kangaroo and *bungwa*, knowing that we were hungry, and as they saw us grow more in want they grew bolder, and at last dragged every stitch off every one of us, and then we were divided amongst the different tribes.

The Lord Mayor: Did it appear to you that they had any idea of religion?

Darge: I could not perceive. If they worshipped anything it was the moon. When it was new they used to dance the *corroburo*. That was all I could observe.

The Lord Mayor: You of course became in some degree acquainted with their language?

Darge: I knew some words. One of the tribes I was with called hungry *corru*, and another nearer to Moreton Bay called it *wiru*. As I became more familiar, they used to exchange names with me, a thing they delighted in. In trying to call me Bob they used to call me Bam, and they used sometimes to call me Garrecia, Moorthema, and Gurmonday, which were some of their own names, and they used to make me call them Bob. Gurmonday was the chief that Mrs Fraser spoke of in the name of Monday.

The Lord Mayor: You don't seem to think these natives such desperate savages as Mrs Fraser and Baxter considered them to be?

Darge: I was certainly treated with great roughness, but I don't think they would kill intentionally.

The Lord Mayor: Then you did not see Captain Fraser killed?

Darge: No, I saw nobody killed. I was separated from Captain Fraser before his death. After I was some time with one of the tribes, I went to another of them, and I was surprised to see two white men amongst them. They were English convicts, and had been in the bush, one of them five years and the other ten years. One of them was called Tursi, and the other, who was a very tall man, named Banks, called himself Tallboy. The first told me he had been cast for death over in England and over in Sydney, and that he had escaped to the bush, where he was determined to live and die, and was perfectly satisfied with his condition. He told me that the tribes were all going to start for the mountains for the honey and the kangaroo, and they remained in the mountains in the summer, and on the beach in the winter. The two white men were like walking skeletons, but they said that they should get quite fat in the mountains, like the black savages, whose appearance also changed very much for the better in the summer months.

The Lord Mayor: Then the wretched criminals who happen to escape to the bush are not safe even in that place of concealment?

Darge: Certainly not; the natives would betray anybody for a *moco* or a *gilla gilla.*

There seem to be no references in the foregoing dialogue to the unhappy relationship between Darge and the Frasers after the shipwreck; Darge, indeed, emerges as a sensible and not insensitive personality. The Lord Mayor sought to attribute the comparative indulgence of the aborigines to the fact that he moved in company with Corralis, a man of colour and thus more acceptable to them. But Darge seems to have had his own way of dealing with their tricky temperaments and it may have been this fact that saved him from the fate of the others. His statement on cannibalism cannot be taken to discount Baxter's evidence; during his escape to Bribie Island he was almost continuously on the move and human meat was by no means an everyday item on the tribesmen's menu.

XV

Publicly Exposed

The London newspapers echoed the Lord Mayor's general feelings of sympathy towards Mrs Fraser (Greene). The public responded, and soon subscriptions were pouring into the Fund. Then came an embarrassing communication. Press reports of the interviews, copied by the provincial newspapers, had come to the attention of a less sympathetic public servant, the Liverpool Commissioner of Police. The arrival of his insinuating letter at the Mansion House must have given Mr Kelly an immediate feeling of entanglement:

Central Police-Office, Liverpool
"MY LORD—*Finding that a person calling herself Mrs Fraser, the widow of the unfortunate master of the* Stirling Castle, *has been making a statement to your Lordship in order to excite the compassion of the humane and obtain money, I think it my duty to acquaint you that she landed here some few weeks back, and applied to me, detailing the same circumstances of distress as those which appear to have interested your Lordship in her behalf. I communicated with the mayor and parochial authorities of the town, who most humanely entered upon the pleasing task of giving her effectual relief; but on the second interview I had with her, an evident exaggeration of her sufferings whilst in captivity, caused a suspicion, and her relief was suspended till inquiries were made, when it turned out that she had married in Sydney, New South Wales, the master of the vessel in which she arrived here, (the* Mediterranean Packet) *who is a man in good circumstances, and who it now appears accompanied her to London (leaving his vessel here in dock), no doubt solely for the*

purpose of raising money by imposing on your Lordship and the public. Her husband, whose name is Greene, is the person who so warm-heartedly confirmed her statement before your Lordship.

Her explanations upon the discovery of her imposition, attempted here, was that her husband (Greene) used her very ill, and she wished to go to London and separate from him; and he, on being sent for, agreed to furnish her with the means to go; after which, however, they remained here some time, and I saw her on more than one occasion elegantly dressed. The mate of the vessel stated that she had a very good wardrobe, and it is certain that, as the wife of Greene, she cannot be in distress.

I am, my Lord, your Lordship's most obedient servant,
M. M. G. Dowling,
Commissioner of Police"

The Lord Mayor of London was clearly in a difficult position. His opposite number in Liverpool, thanks apparently to the perspicacity of his Commissioner of Police, had not been taken in. It seemed that *he* had—when confronted with the letter, the Greenes necessarily admitted they were married. Money had already come in to his Fund and it would be awkward for him to admit soliciting the public for a dubious cause. Hoping to keep the matter quiet, but with the intention of covering himself against future contingencies, the Lord Mayor assembled various documents to establish the main truth of the story.

First on his file was a communication from Mr Wilberforce, a relative of William Wilberforce, and brother-in-law of Stephen Owen, head of the Commissariat at Moreton Bay.

Southampton, August 22nd 1837.
"Mr Wilberforce has the honour of inclosing for the Lord Mayor's inspection a letter, written by Stephen Owen, Esq., an officer in the Commissariat Department stationed at Moreton Bay.

The letter is addressed to Mrs Owen, and relates to the case of Mrs Frazer, which has recently been made known to his Lordship.

As the corner of the letter has been torn, Mr Wilberforce conceives that it may not be improper for him to state, that from his own knowledge of the hand-writing of Mr Owen, who is brother-in-law of Mr Wilberforce, he can positively declare the inclosed letter, and the part of the address on the torn cover, to be the writing of that gentleman."

The note from Owen, dated October 2nd, 1836, included the barest outline of her experience.

"I send you a few lines by Mrs Frazer, who has been passing some time with us; and who has been made a widow on our shores by the cruel hands of the blacks, after suffering shipwreck. Poor Mrs Frazer, after witnessing the death of her husband from the ill-usage of the blacks, had to submit to great cruelties and hardships until, through God's mercy, she was rescued by a party who were sent in search of the shipwrecked crew. Mrs Frazer is about to proceed to her children in Scotland, and should she pass through London on her way, and find an opportunity, she will make you a visit."

Another letter from the Reverend Peter Learmouth, who had been looking after the Fraser children in Stromness, at least confirmed their needy circumstances.

Manse of Stromness, Sept. 1, 1837.
"My Lord,—I hasten to comply with your Lordship's kind request to make you acquainted with the condition and circumstances of the fatherless children concerning whom you write. The oldest is a girl of 16 years, the other two are boys, the one 12 and the other 7 years of age. For nearly two years they have received only £21 for their support, and had it not been that they had, when their mother left them two years ago last May, a little money, they must have been, long ere now, in the greatest destitution. Their money has for some

time been exhausted, and they are now subsisting upon what they received from the grocers here on credit.

Any sum of money which may be contributed for their support by the charitable and benevolent, will be gladly received, and I am sure your Lordship could not have interested yourself on behalf of a family who have a stronger claim upon the sympathy and benevolence of the Christian community. I would humbly suggest to your Lordship that part of the sum of money which may be collected in London may be reserved for the children of Mrs Fraser, and if it be intrusted either to me or the Kirk Session of Stromness, due care will be taken that it is faithfully and judiciously appropriated to their support. In saying this I do not mean to affect the interest of their mother in any respect, whose heart-rending tale of suffering I fully credit.

I would now desire humbly to offer your Lordship my sincere thanks for the interest you have taken in the case of Captain Fraser's family, who, committed as they have been by the providence of God to my care, in circumstances so peculiarly affecting, are fully entitled to whatever exertion I can make to promote their comfort and welfare.

I am, my Lord,
Your Lordship's most humble and obedient servant.
Peter Learmouth"

As additional evidence Baxter produced a letter he had received from his niece, the Fraser daughter in the Orkneys, which for a sixteen-year-old exhibits an impressive piety of style. Her mother had by now been in England for over two months, without having been to see her children.

"I received your kind letter of the 1st of August, dated London, and am happy to hear that you are once more arrived in safety in your native land, as it was more than was expected. I have received a letter from my dear mother, upon her arrival in Liverpool, and I am looking for her daily at Stromness. She intimated that she was to call at London and at Greenock before coming to Orkney. It is

likely that you have seen her before this reaches you. Little was I thinking when at London that it was to be the last interview with my dear father, that I was no more to behold him in this world; but to be taken away from me by death in such a cruel manner by savages! But oh! that we may meet in that heavenly country, where separation is unknown, to sing the song of the Lamb, through the endless ages of eternity. James and David are fine boys, and attend the school closely. Give my kind love to your mother, and aunt Mary, and little Hannah, and may every blessing attend them in this world. David sends his love to his cousin Hannah, with half a dozen kisses. I will write again after my mamma's arrival at Stromness, and give you all the particulars. Uncle John would be very happy to receive a letter from you, to give an account if his son lived a heavenly life, for he received an account of his death.

> *Your affectionate cousin,*
> *Jane Earl Fraser"*

But it was Lieutenant Otter's letter to his sister sent the previous year, a part of which has been quoted (p. 90), that really convinced the Lord Mayor that Mrs Fraser's story of her sufferings was genuine. He had no choice but to be satisfied. In a Solomon-like judgement he ordered that the bulk of the fund should go not to the mother but to the children, to be put into a trust administered by the Kirk authorities in Stromness. Justice seemed to be satisfied, but unhappily it was not allowed to sit back. The *Morning Advertiser*, noted for its aggressive journalism, published Dowling's letter; the Liverpool policeman, disgruntled at the ineffectiveness of his accusations in the capital, had "leaked" the story to the press. Under the headline MRS FRASER, set in bold capitals, it was introduced by a compromising statement: "This person, whose extraordinary adventures among savages have lately excited the sympathy of the public, is now suspected of being an impostor. It appears she is not in distress, but the wife of Greene, the captain of the vessel which brought her to England."

The radical *Morning Post*, taking the opportunity to score a hit against a Tory Lord Mayor, added details that more surely indicates the source of its information: "Upon publicity being given to her revelations before the Lord Mayor, Mr Dowling deemed it his duty to address his Lordship on the subject, acquainting him with the facts just narrated. His Lordship, strange to say, had never taken the slightest notice of Mr Dowling's letter, not even so far as to acknowledge its receipt. Having interested himself very warmly in her behalf, he is probably not anxious to admit that his sympathy has been excited by one entitled to it in a less degree than he at first imagined."

The odious letter, exposing so publicly not only their deception but their private lives, needed some sort of reply, and they must have had difficult moments in its drafting. Mrs Greene's almost casual riposte, presumably master-minded by her husband, neatly avoids the main charge against her, that of concealing her marriage, and tactfully fails to explain why Captain Greene could not have become responsible for the maintenance of his wife and recently acquired step-children.

To the Editor of the Morning Advertiser.

"*Sir,—Glancing over the* Morning Advertiser *of the 27th instant, I observed a copy of a letter that had been transmitted to the Lord Mayor, by a Mr. M. M. G. Dowling, Police Inspector at Liverpool, but to which no date is affixed.*

You will allow me to inform you and the public, that the said letter was received at the Mansion-house about a month since, and that the contents, after having been analysed, did not seem to prejudice the mind of his Lordship against me; neither do I now conclude its having effected a change, though it has now emanated therefrom, and appeared before the public.

With regard to the charges therein against me, I further beg to be permitted to explain the cause which stimulated me to proceed hither, which, I presume, will remove from the public mind every idea of being my an impostor, as the writer impudently alleges.

In the first place, I came to London to ascertain the real position of the late Captain Fraser's affairs, whose transactions with various parties remained open when the Stirling Castle *sailed from the St Katherine's Docks.*

Secondly, my instructions at Sydney, were, on my arrival in Liverpool to proceed to London, appear personally before the Secretary of State for the Colonies, and pray that Government would extend relief to my orphan children.

Immediately after arriving, I proceeded to the Colonial office, but could not obtain an audience with his Lordship, or any further understanding relative to my petition, than that I would be written to in the course of two or three days. After having waited upwards of a week, and receiving no communication whatever therefrom, I at length came to a resolution (as the only alternative remaining) to appear in person before the Right Hon. the Lord Mayor, who, after hearing the detailed narrative of my personal sufferings among the New Hollanders, and the destitution of my orphans, kindly expressed his readiness to be in any wise instrumental to alleviate the distressed circumstances of my family.

I would further observe, that when an appeal was made to public sympathy, it was understood at the Mansion-house that whatever the humane and benevolent community would deposit in the hands of the Lord Mayor would be appropriated solely for the benefit of my three children.

Regarding the writer's allegations against Captain Greene, I would have him know that he is no imposter, neither did he leave his vessel in dock with intention of imposing on the Lord Mayor of the City of London, nor yet the public; but with a view, after having settled his own private affairs, to return to New Zealand.

> *I am, Sir, yours respectfully,*
> *E. A. Greene (late Fraser).*

Sept. 28, 1837."

The Lord Mayor, feeling some sort of public statement to be required, next put out a letter of his own to the press which, as far as he was concerned, brought the matter to a close.

"Mr Editor,—Having observed in the morning papers of the 27th instant the copy of a letter sent from Liverpool to the Lord Mayor, relative to statements made by Mrs Fraser, it becomes necessary, for the satisfaction of those beneficent persons who came forward to alleviate her distresses, to say that the fact of her marriage with Captain Greene was kept back by her on her first application to the Mansion-house, but the Lord Mayor having received a letter from Lieutenant Otter, fully substantiating the account of her sufferings and the murder of her husband (who bore a most excellent character), as well as from the Rev. Peter Learmouth, minister of Stromness, of the destitute state of the three children of Captain Fraser, determined to let the subscription proceed for their benefit; and Mr Learmouth and the Kirk Session have undertaken for the same being dispensed in the manner most conducive to their future welfare, Mrs Greene herself receiving but a moderate sum for necessaries, and to convey her to Stromness.

I am, Sir, your obedient servant,
THOMAS KELLY, *Mayor.*
Mansion-house, Sept. 28."

His Fund had brought in the large sum of £553 7s 2d, the contributions being numerous and varying in amounts from 2s 6d to £26, contributed by the Duke of Devonshire.*

The money was disbursed as follows, and it will be noted that the unlucky Darge got nothing:

---

* Mrs Greene's family name, Britton, is common in Derbyshire where the Duke of Devonshire's main seat, Chatsworth, is located. No doubt members of her family were among his tenants.

	£	s	d.
Cash paid to Mrs Wilkinson for necessaries supplied to Mrs Fraser	1	6	2
Cash paid to Mrs Fraser together with some useful articles of apparel supplied by a lady in Baker Street	50	0	0
Cash transmitted to Rothsay for the use of Mrs Cook, the aged widowed mother of Brown, the chief officer, on whom she depended for support	10	0	0
Cash paid to John Baxter, the second officer	10	0	0
Cash remitted to the Rev. P. Learmouth, and the Kirk Session of Stromness, in Trust for the benefit of the three orphan children of the late Captain Fraser	482	1	0
	£553	7	2*

Curtis, who seems to have acted as a sort of unappointed apologist for both Mrs Greene and the Lord Mayor, wordily sought to exonerate the former from imposition and the latter from any suggestion of credulity.

"A lord mayor," he wrote, "and even personages standing higher on the graduated ladder of 'social compact', from the elevated station which they occupy, must ever expect to become the objects of praise or censure, according to the estimation in which their motives and actions are rated: and they are too often, without cause, subjected to illiberal and ribald attacks, in order to supply with food the vitiated palates of those who seldom exercise the little understanding of which they are masters, either to condemn a bad action or to appreciate a good one.

"With respect to the part which his lordship has taken in regard

* Mrs Greene seems also to have received money from the Treasury, through the personal intervention of Lord Glenelg. Despite his Office's original rejection of her claim, outside pressure—perhaps the news of the Lord Mayor's enquiry—caused him to scrawl urgently on Captain Greene's letter a countermand to the original minute stating that no funds were available:

"Prepare an official version of the enclosed copy to ye Treasury and recommend ye treasury to give the money. Transmit to the Chanc. of Exchq. in person."

to the orphan children of the late Capt. Fraser, we consider it meritorious and praiseworthy, and it was to be expected that he would have been exempted from sarcasm, and shielded from the charge of credulity. We would have those who made that charge know that his lordship is not a gentleman to be easily gulled; on the contrary, he is rather sceptical than otherwise, might almost be deemed fastidious, before he expresses his opinion on any subject. As a magistrate, he has been proverbial for rightly searching after truth in order to ascertain whether deception lurked beneath plausible representations. In the matter now under review, his lordship and his secretaries have been unremitting; and whoever may attempt to rob him of well-earned laurels, the orphan children of Captain Fraser will, doubtless, estimate his kindness so long as they exist.

"His Lordship, who, we believe, acted under the voice of a provisional committee, thought proper to act in the manner he has, in reference to the circumstances which gave rise to his letter, and upon which we offer no further comment.

"We were often in the company of Capt. Greene and his wife, and long before it was known in what relation they stood to each other. It then occurred to us, from the mutual attentions paid, that the lady would at no distant period be Mrs Greene; but in our ignorant speculation, it again occurred to our mind, that her unremitting attention to the gentleman arose from a grateful recollection of favours which he had bestowed in bringing her as an exile from the most distant part of the globe to her native country.

"We are aware that Mrs Greene is charged with great indiscretion in so speedily throwing off the weeds of widowhood. If this be an error, it is one into which many have fallen; as when the proper mate is chosen, ladies as well as gentlemen make the proper time for marrying quite a secondary consideration.

"Here she was in Sydney, in a state bordering on utter destitution. She became acquainted with Capt. Greene, a gentleman well-known and highly respected there, and supposed to be a person in very comfortable circumstances. Perhaps he first viewed her, as did hundreds of others, as an object of commiseration and at length pity gave way to a platonic affection, which ripened into a more tender sensibility.

"Capt. Greene could not have been induced to an alliance with the view of aggrandizement, and therefore we must believe him to have been actuated by a manly and honourable feeling when he entered the sanctuary of God, and solemnly pledged himself to a poor, forlorn, debilitated female, that he would "take her for better for worse", and succour and comfort her all the days of his life.

"Here was Mrs Fraser, a virtuous woman, struggling with adversity, who left all to journey, with the man with whom she had lived in connubial felicity for eighteen years, to the most distant part of another hemisphere, regardless alike of danger and death. Capt. Greene had offered her a passage home in the *Mediterranean Packet* weeks before he proposed the question which had reference to the altar of Hymen. Supposing Mrs Fraser had given a decided negative to that question, and she had sailed a five months' voyage as a "companion", instead of a "wife"—what then? Her virtue would doubtless have been preserved, (for virtuous who can doubt her to have been?) but her reputation probably might not; for even then, superficial readers, deprecating gossips (men as well as women) would have robbed her of her fair fame; and all these, too, emanating from persons who knew nothing of her, and never took the trouble to consider the precarious situation in which she stood.

"We have already conceded that she has acted unwisely in concealing a fact, which, had it been acknowledged, could not have branded either her or her new partner with dishonour; although it might have caused a degree of censure among the slanderers and prudes of the day, yet by some it would have been considered a romantic adventure, and by others a "holy alliance". She has, we admit, acted foolishly in concealing a fact; but that ought to be construed in the most favourable terms. Had she stated, and persisted in a falsehood, then the case would have been different, and she would not have interested the writer of this history in the attempt to palliate her offence. Had that been the case, she would have found no advocate in him, but, as far as he is concerned, would have been left as an object of well-merited contumely.

"Having made these remarks, we beseech our readers to forget her error, which at most is a venial one; and let those who have thought uncharitably of her reflect, that had they been placed in the same circumstances, and surrounded with the same difficulties, and having the same gloomy prospect before them, they might have fallen into the same snare, and entered into a provident, though according to the general notion of the world, a premature and ill-timed alliance. She is fully aware that she has sinned against strict etiquette, and been guilty of an indiscreet secrecy; and we are ready to admit these facts; but without her knowledge, we have attempted an apology."

Curtis does not say on this occasion that he was really of the opinion that she was slightly mad. In addition to his observations on her evidence before the Lord Mayor, he has stated elsewhere: "It appeared evident that the poor woman had evinced symptoms of aberration of mind, and as we have gently hinted, we think we have seen a tendency that way ourselves. And if it be so, who can wonder? Many a lady has found asylum in a mad-house for life in consequence of bereavements less painful—who have never experienced the pains, privations, and insults of the female we are alluding to."

When newspapers containing reports of the Lord Mayor's enquiry and its unpleasant implications reached Sydney some months later, the local press was less tolerant of her behaviour. In a touchy editorial the *Sydney Gazette* contradicted her story that she had no financial aid and warmly defended the Australian national character of hospitality and generosity:

Sydney Gazette. Thursday, January 25, 1838.

THE STIRLING CASTLE

"The recently received British Journals teem with the most horrible accounts of the disastrous wreck of the ship *Stirling Castle* on her voyage from this Colony to Singapore, in May, 1836. Our Colonial readers are sufficiently familiar with the horrifying details of that disastrous occurrence to render any recurrence to the subject unnecessary, our object therefore in referring to the matter now, is not to retrace ground we have already trod, but to undeceive the British public with regard to the statements that, we perceive, have been made before the Lord Mayor of London, and, also to relieve our fellow-colonists from the odium of having displayed an utter want of sympathy for the surviving sufferers, for such is the conclusion which cannot fail to be deduced by the British reader from the narrative published in the British Journals.

"It is not our wish to depreciate the sufferings endured by the wretched survivors, either while exposed, without food and almost without raiment, in an open boat, to the pelting of the pitiless storm, or when forced to endure the brutal tortures of the bloodthirsty savages to the North of Moreton Bay. To these sufferings we do not intend to refer farther than to state that the picture is greatly overcharged, and the various statements made before the Lord Mayor and in this Colony are highly contradictory. The main details, however, are true, and the sufferings endured by Mrs Frazer and the other survivors, undoubtedly entitle her and them to the warmest sympathy of the humane. We do blame Mrs Frazer, however, (and her husband Capt. Greene, late of the *Mediterranean Packet*, at whose instance, doubtless, Mrs F. has gone to London, to lay this statement before the Lord Mayor), for her inexcusable ingratitude in concealing the kindness she met with in Sydney and the very liberal subscription which was made on her behalf previous to her departure. It is impossible for any one, not acquainted with the fact, to read the statements made in the British Newspapers, and not come to the conclusion that the inhabitants of Sydney allowed Mrs Frazer, after a series of such unequalled sufferings, to leave the Colony almost without an expression of sympathy, but certainly without offering her the slightest assistance. So far is this from being the fact, that a subscription was set on foot, and, if we mistake not, upwards of £400 was presented to Mrs Frazer, before her departure from Sydney, or her marriage to Captain Greene.

"We do not blame Mrs Frazer for wishing to excite the sympathy of the British public in her behalf, but that object, we conceive, might have been attained as well without any concealment of the truth. Captain Greene's conduct in the matter is highly reprehensible if he, as is stated in the Journals before us, not only concealed the fact of his marriage altogether, but stated that 'the unfortunate lady was not mistress of a farthing.'

"It is too late now to prevent the British public from being imposed on, but it is not too late to remove an impression injurious to our national character, which cannot fail to be caused by the perusal of such horrible details, accompanied by the entire concealment of the treatment Mrs Frazer experienced in Sydney."

It is difficult to assess to what extent the poor lady was responsible for her shady actions. Her experiences on the 'Fatal Shore' had clearly been more than her temperament and constitution could stand and Captain Greene, who should have been her protector, seems only to have been her exploiter. The last glimpse we have of her is provided by Henry Stuart Russell.*

"Walking down Hyde Park from Oxford Street, I observed a man who was carrying over his shoulder one of those show advertisements: a large wooden frame nailed to the end of a long pole. On the calico with which it was covered was a bright daub which represented savages with bows and arrows, some dead bodies of white men and women, which other savages were cutting up on the ground, and another squad were holding 'spits' to a large fire. It was amusing enough to stop my walk: horrible

* *Genesis of Queensland* (Turner & Henderson, 1888).

enough to impress the writing beneath the picture on my mind—
'STIRLING CASTLE' WRECKED OFF THE COAST OF NEW HOL-
LAND, BOTANY BAY, ALL KILLED AND EATEN BY SAVAGES:
ONLY SURVIVOR A WOMAN: TO BE SEEN: 6D. ADMISSION.

With her Captain checking receipts in the background, we can
imagine her sitting in some crude booth against a painted tropic
backcloth, perhaps exposing her more available scars to a prurient
public and declaiming a lurid summary of her misadventures.
Her display before the aborigines at Lake Cootharaba can hardly
have been less edifying.

Epilogue

Information from descendants in New Zealand indicates that Captain and Mrs Greene and the Fraser children finally settled in Auckland. Captain Greene invested some of his wife's money in land, an unsuccessful venture, as it was later found that the titles had lapsed. James, the elder Fraser boy, was apprenticed to Captain Greene and finally became a sea captain himself. He died in 1906 having had nine children. The daughter, Jane, married James Stephens of Los Angeles, who later became Attorney General for California. Eliza Greene apparently died in Melbourne in 1858, said to have been killed in a carriage accident.

Appendix I

Lines addressed by Captain Fraser to his wife written in an open boat after the wreck of the *Comet* in the Torres Strait.

My heart is sick, and bones are sore,
    As I'm toss'd on the raging sea,
My anxious mind can find no rest,
    Thinking, my dear, on thee.
Through travelling far in search of gain,
    Our toils are all in vain,
Our good-like barque's wrecked on a reef,
    And there she must remain.
Her frame was stout—her beams were strong,
    Her bow kept to the sea,
The billows beat with all their strength,
    Her timbers for to free
For two long days and two long nights
    She stagger'd to and fro,
At last her frame it must give way,
    And our hearts were fill'd with woe.
Our only hope was in the boats,
    And God's protecting care,
Our lives to save and cross the reef,
    All hearts were filled with fear.
Now farewell, *Comet*, for we must leave,
    Thy sailing's now all o'er,
Thou was a fam'd and gallant barque,
    And at Sydney much ador'd.

Two lambs are left on board of thee,
    Which I'm sorry for at heart,
A cat and parrot nursed by me,
    For which I had a great regard.

Appendix II

A case of cannibalism among convicts.

Alexander Pierce was the last survivor of a party of six runaways who had successively killed and eaten each other. This experience seems to have given him a taste for human flesh, for he absconded a second time with the following grisly results as quoted in the Appendix to Report from the Select Committee on Transportation (1838).

"Alexander Pierce and Thomas Cox absconded from Macquarie Harbour on the 16th November 1823. On the 21st November, as the *Waterloo* was sailing down the harbour, some of the pilot's crew observed a man on the beach making a signal by smoke; Mr Lucas sent his boat ashore in consequence. The same signal was observed from the settlement from which a boat was also sent, both boats returned before dark, bringing with them Alexander Pierce, who had confessed having murdered his fellow-prisoner, Thomas Cox, two days before, and that he had lived upon his body ever since. A piece of human flesh, about half-a-pound, was found upon his person. Pierce told Lieutenant Cuthbertson all the particulars of the murder, and that he would point out the unfortunate Cox's remains.

"A boat was accordingly dispatched with Pierce early next morning for King's River, well guarded. After the party landed, and had walked about 400 yards by Pierce's directions, the body was found and brought to the settlement in a dreadfully mangled state being cut right in two at the middle, the head off, the private parts torn off, all the flesh off the calves of the legs, back of the thighs and loins, also off the thick part of the arms, which the inhuman wretch declared was most delicious food; none of the intestines were found; he said that he threw them behind a tree, after having roasted and devoured the heart and a part of the liver; one of the hands was also missing.

"Pierce would not be in want of food when he committed this horrid deed, as he had been then only three days from the settlement, and had some flour with him when they absconded and further, when he was taken there was found upon his person a piece of pork, some bread, and a few fish, which he had plundered from a party of hunters two days before, but which he had not tasted, stating that human flesh was by far preferable.

"On being questioned why he murdered Cox, he said that they quarrelled about the route they were to pursue, and Cox being the strongest man, he was obliged to take up an axe, with which he knocked him down and killed him.

"His reason for giving himself up was, that he had no hope of ultimately escaping, and that he was so horror-struck at his own inhuman conduct, and that he did not know what he was about when he made the signal on the beach. He had on the murdered man's clothes when brought back to the settlement. He was sent to Hobart Town, per *Waterloo* 21st November 1823, tried for the murder, and executed."

In 1832 the convicts Edward Broughton and Mathew Maccavoy were hanged "for the wilful Murder of three of their Fellow Transports and eating them as Food".

Appendix III

Missionaries come to Moreton Bay. The *Stirling Castle* disaster was later to be used as an argument in favour of establishing missionaries north of Moreton Bay, as the following letter indicates.

Rev. Dr. Lang to Sir George Grey.
London. 12 May 1837.

Sir,—With reference to a paragraph of my letter (of the 23rd January last) as to whether His Majesty's Government would grant assistance from the colonial revenue of New South Wales, for the establishment and maintenance of a mission to the aborigines of that colony, undertaken by the Presbyterian Church, I have the honour to state that, in consequence of the present demand for ministers of that communion for the white population of the colony, it has been deemed inexpedient to send out any presbyterian minister at present as a missionary to the aborigines, as the probability is, that on his arrival in the colony he would be solicited to become the master of a congregation of Europeans, and be induced to forego his proper work and office as a missionary to the heathen.

With the view, therefore, of ensuring the permanency and success of a mission to the aborigines of New South Wales, to be established under the auspices and management of the colonial presbyterian communion, acting in concert with the Church of Scotland and the Synod of Ulster, it has been deemed expedient at the outset to solicit the aid and co-operation of the evangelical portion of the Lutheran Church of the Continent, which, as you are aware, approximates so closely in its doctrines, disciplines, and forms of worship to the Church of Scotland, as in certain states of Germany, as in Prussia, for example, to coalesce entirely with the reformed or presbyterian communion; I have accordingly been enabled, on behalf of the Presbyterians of New South Wales and Van Diemen's Land, with whose sentiments on this subject I am well acquainted, to engage, for the establishment of a mission to the aborigines at Moreton Bay, the three following missionaries of the Lutheran communion, all of whom have expressed their entire willingness to submit themselves, in all matters of discipline, as well as in everything relating to the general management of the proposed mission, to the ecclesiastical jurisdiction of the colonial Presbyterian Church; viz. Messrs Christopher Eipper and Gottlob Schreiner, both natives of the kingdom of Wertemberg; also Candidate Schmidt, a native of Prussia, Frederick Franz, Peter Niqué, Gottfried Hausman, Joachim Holzhausen, August Rhode, Lundarg Döge, August Olbrecht, Moritz Schneider, Gottlieb Hartenstein and Gottfried Wagner, all of whom, though originally of the class of operatives or mechanics, have for a considerable time past been under training and desirous of being employed in any capacity for the welfare of the heathen.

As the only missionary stations at present occupied in the colony are Lake Macquarie, on the coast about fifty miles northward of Sydney, Wellington Valley, in the interior, and very recently Port Philip, I beg most respectfully to submit to your attention and consideration the extreme importance of Moreton Bay as an additional station, as well as endeavouring, by a comparatively extensive and well-directed missionary agency, to make a strong impression on the tribes to the northward. While the natives are comparatively numerous in the vicinity of Moreton Bay, the frequency of shipwrecks on the reefs, to the northward of that settlement, is ever and anon exposing the helpless Europeans who survive these disasters to the savage brutality of the tribes on the coast; and it is only by extending missionary operations from Moreton Bay, as the point of departure, along the coast to the northwards, that these tribes can be subjected to the humanising influences of Christian civilisation. My own father and twelve other persons were lost in a small vessel on the coast seven years ago and may possibly still be alive in the hands of the savages. But a case of much more recent occurrence will, I trust, induce the Right Honourable Secretary of State for the Colonies to grant the need of assistance towards the establishment of the proposed mission at Moreton Bay, which I have done myself the honour to solicit. The Stirling Castle, a vessel in which I made a voyage to the colony, and carried several ministers of religion and instructors of youth, has recently been wrecked on a reef, and the captain and first officer, and several of the crew, barbarously murdered by the black natives to the northward of that settlement, after escaping safely in their boats to the shore.

I have the honour etc.
John Dunmore Lang.

Appendix IV

Aboriginal methods of preparing dead bodies.

A detailed description of their principles and processes has been given by the Reverend Dr Lang in his book *Cooksland* (1842). Lang had most of his facts from "Durrambhoi" Davies, an escaped convict who lived for seventeen years among the aborigines.

"When the dead body of a person who has either fallen in battle, or had died a natural death, is to be subjected to this horrid process, it is stretched out on its back, and a fire lighted on each side of it. Firebrands are then passed carefully over the whole body, till its entire surface is thoroughly scorched. The cuticle, consisting of the epidermis or scarfskin, and the reticulum mucosum, or mucous membrane of Malpighi, in which the colouring matter of the skin is contained, is then peeled off, sometimes with pointed sticks, sometimes with mussel-shells, and sometimes even with the finger nails, and then placed in a basket or dilly to be preserved. And as the cutis vera, or true skin, is, in all varieties of the human family, perfectly white, the corpse then appears of that colour all over; and I have no doubt whatever, that it is this peculiar and ghastly appearance which the dead body of a black man uniformly assumes under this singular treatment, and with which the aborigines must be quite familiar wherever the practice obtains, that has suggested to them the idea that white men are merely their forefathers returned to live again; the supposition that particular white men are particular deceased natives, known to the Aborigines when alive, being merely this idea carried out to its natural result, under the influence of a heated imagination. There is reason also to believe, *e converso*, that wherever this idea prevails, the practice in which it has originated—that of peeling off the cuticle previous to the other parts of the process to be described hereafter—is still prevalent also, or has been so, at least, very recently.

"After the dead body has been subjected to the process of scorching with firebrands, it becomes so very stiff as almost to be capable of standing upright of itself. If the subject happens to be a male, the subsequent part of the process is performed by females, but if a female, it is performed by males. The body is then extended upon its face, and certain parties, who have been hitherto sitting apart in solemn silence (for the whole affair is conducted with the stillness of a funeral solemnity), step forward, and with a red pigment, which shows very strongly upon the white ground, draw lines down the back and along the arms from each shoulder down to the wrist. These parties then retire, and others who have previously been sitting apart in solemn silence, step forward in like manner, and with sharp shells cut through the cutis vera, or true skin, along these lines. The entire skin of the body is then stripped off in one piece, including the ears and the finger-nails, with the scalp, but not the skin of the face which is cut off. This whole process is performed with incredible expedition, and the skin is then stretched out on two spears to dry, the process being sometimes hastened, by lighting a fire under the skin. Previous to this operation, however, the skin is restored to its natural colour, by being anointed all over with a mixture of grease and charcoal.

"When the body has thus been completely flayed, the dissectors step forward and cut it up. The legs are first cut off at the thighs, then each arm at the shoulder, and last of all the head; not a drop of blood appearing during the process. The larger sections are then subdivided and portioned out among the expectant multitude, each of whom takes his portion to one or other of the fires, and when half-roasted devours it with great apparent relish. The flesh of the natives in the northern country generally is very fat, and that of children, which are never skinned like adults, particularly so. Davies has often seen a black fellow holding his portion of his fellow-creature's dead body to the fire in one hand, on a branch or piece of wood stuck through it like a fork or skewer, with a shell or hollow piece of bark under it in the other, to receive the melted fat that dropped from it, and drinking it up when he had caught a sufficient quantity to form a draught, with the greatest gusto. In this way the body disappears with incredible rapidity, the bones being very soon cleaned of every particle of flesh.

"The bones are then carefully collected, and placed in a dilly or basket, and forwarded by a trusty person to all the neighbouring tribes, in each of which they are mourned over successively, for a time, by those to whom the deceased was known. They are then returned to the tribe to which the deceased belonged, and carried about by his relatives for months, or even years, till at length they are deposited permanently in a hollow tree, from which it is esteemed unpardonable sacrilege to remove it."

Appendix V

Concerning the dugong.

Dugong. Order of *sirenia*, a mammal related to the manatee of South America. Sometimes known as a "sea-cow", the dugong is a seal-like animal 8 ft to 10 ft long weighing about 1,200 lbs. It has thick, fleshy lips and heavy bones to enable it to feed on weeds at the bottom of the sea. The habit of the female holding her baby to her breast with a flipper while surfacing for air or feeding in a human manner, together with the fish-like tail, is said to have inspired the mermaid myth, though the hairy-mouthed dugong cannot have aroused many romantic feelings in the early seamen.

Tin-Can or Tindchin Creek, opposite Fraser Island, was a great place for hunting by the aborigines and the name is said to be a corruption of *Yuangan*, the local word for the dugong. The supply was shortly to decrease drastically; immigrant enterprise became aware of the value of dugong oil for medicinal purposes and this interesting species soon became a commercial proposition—200 gallons of oil were exported in 1858–59. An article published in 1862 gives an analogy between dugong hunting and cattle ranching.

"Upon the island of St Helena, in Moreton Bay, the first submarine run has been formed, and is now in the second season of its operations, under the superintendence of an experienced person formerly engaged in the seal trade in Newfoundland. Around this lovely island, for miles in every direction, are extensive submarine pastures of great luxuriance, affording a never-failing supply of long grass, upon which the herds of dugong feed and fatten like oxen on the plains. For seven months of the year these animals are taken almost daily, by means of long nets across the channel leading to and from their feeding grounds.

"A large boiler, capable of holding one of these monsters is continually steaming away, and the oil flows away from a tap in the upper part of the boiler in a clear limpid stream, the colour of pale sherry wine. Upon cooling the oleine and stearine separate. The latter is sold to soap makers for about £40 a ton; while the former is used for medical purposes as a substitute for cod liver oil."

An article in the Brisbane Courier in 1869 said that herds of dugong "in almost incredible numbers" were to be found in Moreton Bay, Wide Bay, Hervey Bay and Rodd's Bay. The flesh was described as tasting like "splendid veal cutlets".

Inefficient methods of production led to a decline in the trade, but it was revived more effectively in World War Two, when thousands were slaughtered for their oil. Today the dugong is rare in Queensland, though numbers can be seen congregating off Fraser Island, where the author noted a rusty boiler in the undergrowth. The dugong is now protected in Australia, though the aborigines are allowed to kill them for food.

Appendix VI

The Bunya-Bunya Pine.

Only rumours of the fabled bunya-bunya *Aurucaria bidwilii* had reached white men, other than those living with the tribes, at this time. It was not until 1838 that Andrew Petrie, Foreman of the Works at Brisbane and an amateur naturalist and anthropologist, visited its ranges, made a drawing of it and brought back a sample of timber. But the honour of naming it went, perhaps unfairly, to John Carne Bidwill (1815–1853) of the Botanical Society of London and a Director of the Botanic Gardens, Sydney. He was later taken up into the bunya-bunya district by Henry Stuart Russell, where he dug up three seedlings and despatched them to London in a Wardian case. One went to Kew, where a specimen of the tree can today be seen growing in the Temperate greenhouse, and another to Chatsworth. Russell could remember cones being sold at Covent Garden for five guineas each.

According to Petrie "this tree grows to an immense girth and height. I have measured some ordinary sized trees, 150 feet high and about four feet in diameter. They are straight and round as a gun-barrel. The timber grows in spiral form, and would answer admirably for ships' masts of any size. This pine bears a great strain transversely, one of its superior qualities; also there is no sap wood nor knots in the barrel, the lateral branches never being above two or three inches in diameter and growing from the outer rind of the tree. The fruit of this pine is a large cone or core, about nine inches by six, and covered in small cones similar in appearance to a pine-apple. It is these small nuts that the blacks eat; they travel two or three hundred miles to feed on this fruit. It is plentiful every three years. This timber grows in latitude 25° and 26° and about 60 miles in longitude. It is not known at present to grow anywhere else. I was the first person who risked my life with others in procuring the first plants of this tree and Bidwill was some years after me."

In a letter to his friend Robert Lynd, the explorer Leichhardt, the first man to travel overland from Moreton Bay to Port Essington on the northern extremity of the continent (1844–5), described the role of the tree in aboriginal life:

"I have travelled again in those remarkable mountain brushes, out of which the Bunya-Bunyas lift their majestic heads, like pillars of the blue vault of Heaven. I measured several, and their circumference six feet high was 17 to 20 feet. The black-fellows go up to the top of these giants of vegetation with a simple bushvine, which they put round the tree and which they push higher with every step they take upwards. They break the cones, almost a foot long and 9 inches in diameter, and throw them down. They whistle through the air and their fall sounds far through the silence of the brush. Those trees the fruit of which we gathered had 4, 5 or 6 cones. Every cone contained, perhaps 40 to 50 fertile scales; many, and particularly those at the top of the cone, are not fertile. The black-fellows eat an immense quantity; and indeed, it is difficult to cease, if one has once commenced to eat them. If you find a favourable tree, and if the circumstances are favourable too,—for instance if the day is cool, in the morning and evening,—the kernel of the Bunya fruit has a very fine aroma, and it is certainly a delicious eating; but during a very hot day or from an unfavourable tree, the fruit is by no means so tasteful as I hoped to find them generally. The black-fellows roast them, and we tried even to boil them; the fruit lost, however, its flavour in both cases. Besides, it did not agree with my stomach. (They are slightly cathartic.) The black-fellows thrive well on them, but Mr Archer told me that the young people return generally with boils all over their body."

In the opinion of the author the *bunya-bunya* is not an especially elegant tree, and for some reason Petrie does not describe the sadly drooping branches and their thorny excrescences. The nuts, however, are delicious.

Appendix VII

Moreton Bay Settlement in 1836.

Moreton Bay settlement, which has grown into modern Brisbane, had been moved six miles upstream from its original site. It then consisted of nothing more than the appurtenances of a penal station. Earlier that year the Settlement had been visited by two Quakers, James Backhouse and George Washington Walker. Shown round by the Commandant, Captain Foster Fyans, they wrote an account of their impressions:

"Adjacent to the Government House are the Commandant's garden and 22 acres of Government gardens for the growth of sweet potatoes, cabbages, and other vegetables for the prisoners. Bananas, grapes, guavas, pineapples, citrons, lemons, shaddocks, etc., thrive luxuriantly in the open ground. The climate being nearly tropical, sugar canes are grown for fencing, and there are a few thriving coffee plants, but not old enough to bear fruit. The treadmill is generally worked by twenty-five prisoners at a time but, when it is used as a special punishment, sixteen are kept upon it fourteen hours, with only the interval of release afforded by four being off at a time. Many of the prisoners were occupied in landing cargoes of maize or Indian corn from a field down the river and others in divesting it of the husks. To our regret, we heard an officer swearing at the men and using other improper and exasperating language. We visited the prisoners' barracks—a large stone building calculated to accommodate 1,000 men, but now occupied by 311. We also visited the penitentiary for female prisoners, seventy-one of whom are here . . . employed in washing, needlework, picking oakum and nursing." (op. cit., Cilento & Lack.)

Appendix VIII

A convict's lament on the death of Captain Logan.

I am a native of the land of Erin,
 And lately banished from that lovely shore;
I left behind my aged parents,
 And the girl I did adore.
In transient storms as I set sailing,
 Like mariner bold my course did steer;
Sydney Harbour was my destination—
 That cursed place at length drew near.

I then joined banquet in congratulation
 On my safe arrival from the briny sea;
But, Alas, Alas! I was mistaken—
 Twelve years transportation to Moreton Bay.
Early one morning, as I carelessly wandered,
 By the Brisbane waters I chanced to stray;
I saw a prisoner sadly bewailing,
 Whilst on the sunlit banks he lay.

He said: "I've been a prisoner at Port Macquarie,
 At Norfolk Island, and Emu Plains;
At Castle Hill and cursed Toongabbee—
 At all those places I've worked in chains,
But of all the places of condemnation,
 In each penal station of New South Wales,
Moreton Bay I found no equal,
 For excessive tyranny each day prevails.

Early in the morning, as the day is dawning,
  To trace from heaven the morning dew,
Up we are started at a moment's warning,
  Our daily labour to renew.
  Our overseers and superintendents—
  These tyrants' orders we must obey,
Or else at the triangles our flesh is mangled—
  Such are our wages at Moreton Bay!

For three long years I've been beastly treated;
  Heavy irons each day I wore;
My poor back from flogging has been lacerated,
  And oftimes painted with crimson gore.
Like the Egyptians and ancient Hebrews,
  We were sorely oppressed by Logan's yoke,
Till kind Providence came to our assistance,
  And gave this tyrant his fatal stroke.

Yes, he was hurried from that place of bondage,
  Where he thought he would gain renown;
But a native black, who lay in ambush,
  Gave this monster his fatal wound,
Fellow prisoners, be exhilarated;
  Your former sufferings you will not mind,
For it's when from bondage you are extricated,
  You'll leave such tyrants far behind!"

STATE OF CONVICTS,
In New South Wales, 1835.

THE true nature of the Punishment of TRANSPORTATION is not sufficiently known, or it is too slightly thought of by those who are living in a state of continual crime. To such persons this Paper is addressed, with the hope that it may induce them to reflect, and check their guilty practices before they bring down upon themselves the infliction of the violated Laws of their Country. T.

Extract from a LETTER written by a Convict, in the 9th. year of his banishment, to a Gentleman in London, dated Montpelier, New South Wales.

"AS regards the State of the Prison Population I have much to say. The Discipline of this Colony has become dreadfully severe; *every year* has increased its severity since I have been here.——Disobedience or insolence is *fifty lashes*—first offence not less than twenty-five; second offence *seventy-five* or *a hundred lashes;* third offence twelve months to an *Iron Gang.* Absconding —or Taking-the-Bush, as we term it—is *fifty lashes* first offence; second time TWELVE MONTHS to an IRON GANG, and increased each offence.

"Nothing is more dreaded by the men than Iron Gangs; as when their sentence is expired they have *all that time spent in irons to serve again,* as every sentence is now in addition to the original sentence. If a man is nearly due for his ticket of leave, and is flogged, he is put back for a certain time, unless for theft, and then he forfeits every indulgence. If an iron-gang man has served any number of years in the country, he must begin again; he is the same as a new hand; he has to wait the whole term of years before he receives any indulgence. Now to judge properly of the Punishment I have mentioned, you may ask,—What is the Punishment adopted in Iron Gangs? It is this. The delinquents are employed in forming new roads, by cutting through mountains, blasting rocks, cutting the trees up by the roots, felling and burning off. They are attended by a Military Guard, night and day, to prevent escape; wear Irons upon both legs, and at night are locked up in small wooden houses, containing about a dozen sleeping places; escape is impossible; otherwise they live in huts surrounded by high paling, called stockades; they are never allowed after labour to come without the stockade under penalty of being shot; so complete is the confinement, that not half-a-dozen have escaped within the last two or three years; they labour from one hour after sunrise until eleven o'clock, then two hours to dinner and work until night; no supper. The triangles are constantly at hand to tie up any man neglecting work, or insolent. Iron-Gang Men not allowed to be hut keepers, cooks, or other occupation, as such is considered an indulgence; nothing but hard labour. Not one day of liberty will he ever enjoy; *he will have all his sentences in addition to his original sentence to serve again.* Picture to yourself this hot climate, the labour and the ration, and judge for yourself if there is laxity of discipline. It is to places such as I have described, that the Judges now sentence men from the English bar—poor wretches! did they know their fate, be assured, respected Sir, it had been well for them had they never been born." "H. W. D.

Appendix X

Lieutenant Otter's Report.

To Captain Foster Fyans. Commandant, Moreton Bay.
27th August, 1836.

"Sir,—In compliance with your desire, I have the honour to state for the information of His Excellency, the circumstances through which I became acquainted with the wreck of the *Stirling Castle* and the further steps which I took in pursuance of your instructions to rescue a part of the crew who were in the hands of the Natives.

"On Monday the 8th Inst., after having visited the Pilot Station, I proceeded for a day to Breiby's Island at the north of the Bay, previous to returning to the settlement—I arrived there on Tuesday and whilst out shooting in the afternoon, two men were brought up to me whom I at first took to be Natives as they were quite black and perfectly naked. When they came up they told me that they belonged to the Brig *Stirling Castle* which had left Sydney for Singapore in the middle of May last, and that she had been wrecked on one of the barrier reefs near the entrance of Torres Straits six days after she sailed, that the whole crew had got off the wreck eleven of them in the long boat and seven in the Pinnace. That after keeping together for some time, the Pinnace left them as she was the fastest boat and they saw no more of her. That the long boat in which were the Captain, his wife, two Mates and seven hands, stood on to the Southward for about a fortnight after parting company with the Pinnace, that they were then forced to beach her about twenty miles to the

Southward of Sandy Cape, after enduring great suffering and privation for the want of water, that they had subsequently been stripped and cruelly used by the Natives, that two of their number had been drowned in endeavouring to swim the channel which separated them from the Main, and that they themselves with another man (who had been forced to stop about 25 miles behind) had proceeded along the beach from tribe to tribe for five weeks, and after undergoing a variety of hardships, arrived at Breiby's Island and most fortunately fell in with us. I immediately sent two of the boat's crew in quest of the man who had been left behind and they brought him back about 12 o'clock the following day when I immediately returned to the Settlement.

"On Thursday the 11th inst., I started by your direction with the two whale boats, in quest of the remainder of the crew and arrived at the Pilot Station the same night. The next day we reached the Northern port of Breiby's Island, and on Saturday arrived in Huon Mundy's river about 50 miles to the Northward. As we expected some intelligence at this place, and as no natives appeared, I dispatched the prisoner Graham to one of their camps, with the situation of which he was well acquainted— about 8 o'clock at night a number of lights were perceived coming along the beach on the opposite side of the river. I crossed over to meet them and on coming up, had the satisfaction of finding that Graham had succeeded in getting two of the men who were accompanied by about 20 of the natives. He informed us that the Captain (Fraser) and the first mate had sunk under the hardships to which they were exposed, that they had left Mrs Fraser about five days ago when she was still alive though suffering dreadfully from the cruelty of the natives and that she was somewhere on the main beach in Wide Bay, while the second mate still remained on the island.

"The next morning (Sunday) I dispatched one of the boats round Double Island Point, the southern extremity of Wide Bay, about 40 miles distant, with directions to beach her in the first convenient place they could find. Whilst I proceeded with

Graham and two other men by land, as I thought there might be some chance of our hearing of her on the road. As the natives who brought the men in had shewn them more kindness than any other tribe, I distributed a few tomahawks amongst them, and they accompanied us along the beach. When we had gone about six miles, they all rushed into the bush and having provided themselves with waddies, they immediately attacked and endeavoured to surround us. As it was a principal object to avoid alarming the natives I had taken no muskets with us, we were therefore obliged to return to the boat, as they shewed very little fear of our pistols though we fired two or three shots, which hereby seemed to keep them off.

"When we got back I started directly for Wide Bay which I reached before night and joined the other boat. The following morning (Monday) Graham started off to obtain intelligence and returned the following day with the second mate whom he had brought off the island in a native canoe. He had made every inquiry for Mrs Fraser, and was told that, in the hope of getting to the Southward she had followed some natives who were going to fight another tribe about 35 miles off. As he told me he knew the exact spot they were gone to, he started again the same afternoon, and I followed him early the next morning with the two Corporals (Campbell and McGuire) and Mitchell the cockswain, all of us well armed for the purpose of rendering any assistance that might be required. After walking about 25 miles we found a mark in the sand, which had been previously agreed upon as a sign to halt. We had not been there more than half an hour when Graham appeared with four natives and gave us the gratifying intelligence that he succeeded, and that Mrs Fraser was waiting close at hand for a cloak to cover her, as she had been stripped by the natives from the very first as well as the rest. She came to us in a few minutes after and though dreadfully debilitated and crippled from the sufferings she had undergone, she insisted upon starting instantly for the tents, which indeed it became prudent to do as there were nearly 300 natives assembled in a camp about 9 miles off, many of whom had been very unwilling to give her up. We accordingly proceeded on our return and managed by occasionally carrying her to reach the boats about 3 o'clock the following morning. Having now recovered all that survived of the long-boat's crew, we endeavoured to get away on Friday but were forced to put back. On the following Sunday we again doubled the point and a fair wind springing up we were enabled by standing on all night to reach the settlement the following Evening.

"I cannot conclude without requesting that I may be allowed to recommend to His Excellency's notice, the prisoner Graham to whose indefatigable exertions we are indebted for our success. He shunned neither danger nor fatigue, and on the last occasion he was exposed to very imminent risk, by venturing into the large Camp where Mrs Fraser was detained, as had he met there any of the natives who attacked us a few days before it might have been fatal to him—as he was obliged not only to go unarmed, but to strip himself perfectly naked when he went amongst them.

"I am sorry to say that one of the gig's crew (Shannon) was speared through the thigh whilst cutting fire wood within 100 yards of our camp, by some of the natives, who were continually watching us.

I have the honor to be
        Sir
Your most obedt Humb. Servt.
        C. Otter Lt.
        4th (Kings Own) Regt."

Appendix XI

Graham's Memorandum.

"Memorandum of the real facts—follows of John Graham etc:

That I was tryed and sentenced at Dundalk March the 4th 1824. Arrived per Hooghley the 1st of July 1825 and was Tryed and Sentenced the 28th of October 1826, at Sydney 7 years to Moretain bay. That being forwarded to moreton bay Decbr. 1826, being Induced to abscond in July 1827 where I remaind a fugitive among the natives north of moreton bay till 1833 when he returned to moreton bay the 1st of Novembr. and got his liberty when it pleasd Capt Clunie to take his freedom from him on the 16th of Novmbr 1833 and since paying up the Time he was absent after an act of Counsil passed May 1830 Though to me unknown That proffered Rewards and Promises from Capt Fyans Commandant at moreton bay he volunteered to go search The mountains of the north among the Canibals and savages, for the survivors of the Sterling Castle where the blacks had carried them with the wife of the murdered Capt. Fraser which they had for a show That going 200 miles in 2 boats 20 of a party Lieutenant Otter being Commander the party was forced to lie by there boats as the Savages kept anoying them throwing Sticks and spears and John Shannon was Speard trough the thigh Several Spears been thrown at the party the were forcd to fire to frighten Them That John Graham here was forcd to venture every thing by himselfe not only to Save the lives of the party but the lives of the unhappy people they had carried away—That on the 13th of august he freed Robert Cary and Robert Demon from the Savages

181

at Lake Fyans That on 15th he freed John Baxter from 300 savages on McClays Island and went over 4 mile of watter on the mouth of Cousks bay for him That on The 7th of august 1836, he freed Mrs Fraser from seven hundred Canniballs and savages who had her in the mountains (as a show) west of Cousks wide Lake Where he went and getting the tribes that claimed him as There friend to Stand by him while he claimed her as him or the (Spirit of his wife) he succeeded to take her from thoes frightful Clans—and hoards of Canniballs and savages and carried her upwards of 40 miles with the assistance of 4 blacks that came with him from the mountains and by traveling all the knight he reatched the boats at wide bay on the morning of Thursday 18th of august 1836. and thus by himself risqued all and freed all not as has been stated That his Superior knowledge of the country and Language kept them all from harm and even the Savage from being killed after all Thoes promises I am still detained and after venturing my life to save and face the waves in open boats after Delivering four Christians from the Canniballs and savage what no other person would do i hope to be rewarded.

I humbly hope that something may be done.
Yours etc.
John Graham."

Appendix XII

"On Captain Fraser's Child born in a boat."

"Poor Babe! how tempestuous, how stormy thy pillow;
Asleep on the surge of the rough mountain billow.
Like the world, all around thee was fearful commotion,
So comfortless toss'd on this life's dreary ocean.

'Born in sin' in a world that refuses a pillow,
'No rest' for the soul 'midst the surf of life's billow;
Confusion, and sorrow, and warfares are waging,
While hurricanes madly around us are raging.

Yet I had a bosom, and soft was the pillow,
My MOTHER provided far off from each billow;
Her tears and her prayers, and maternal tuition,
Procured me, through grace, all my present fruition.

How brief was thy voyage, how rough was thy pillow,
Just launched in the sea, and then borne on a billow;
Fit emblem of life, with its ten thousand sorrows,
Through sin and the curse in the world's dreary horrors.

How quickly the haven of glory they pillow,
Received thy blest spirit far off from the billow;
Blood ransom'd by Jesus, through grace so abounding,
The throne of his glory with INFANTS surrounding.

(Published in "The Soldiers and Sailors Magazine".)

Ah! there was a Babe with a manger his pillow,
A stable his birth-place on life's rudest billow;
In 'swaddling clothes' wrapt' midst infernal commotion,
To sink and to die on live's accurst ocean.

Then Jesus provided for INFANTS a pillow,
In heaven, where storms and the wild raging billow;
No more shall distress or alarm, but salvations,
On Abram's bosom sing redeemed of all nations."

Appendix XIII

Poem written to Captain Fraser when a young man
by his sister.

A Sister's Advice

Accept, dear James, from thy most anxious friend,
Some useful counsel by affection penn'd.
To my advice you've oft indifference paid,
Which bids me hope this last will be obeyed.
Then, my dear brother, kindly plead excuse
For every error in your sister's muse.
First, my young sailor, let me recommend
In life's fair spring to make your God your friend.
That Power which you in bloom of youth engage,
Will ne'er desert you in declining age.
Unto your mother every reverence pay,
'Tis God's command her precepts to obey.
Be duteous, tender, open and sincere:
She then shall love thee, and they name revere.
Be firm in friendship—scorn all mean disguise,
Nor suffer mean resentment to arise.
Beware of passion, it unmans the soul,
If once indulged, it never brooks control.
Temperance, dear James, I warmly recommend,
In fumes of wine too oft is lost a friend.
Trembling I charge thee, fatal gambling shun,
A desperate vice, which thousands have undone!
Oh! fly the frenzy with contempt and scorn;

Though made at night, reflection comes with morn.
Of wedlock's state I can but little say,
For youthful hearts in general take their way:
I only raise to Hymen's throne my voice,
That he may lead you to a happy choice.
Dear as you are—detested be your name,
If ere you bring the innocent to shame,
Or stain the honour of a virtuous race,
Or bring a hapless female to disgrace.
Scorn not their ruin—every aid pray lend,
For man was made their honour to defend.
When we're apart—thou on some distant shore,
Think on the writer, and these lines read o'er.
They are her counsels, and with hope sincere,
She trusts James Fraser will to them adhere.
Then will his fame ever unclouded shine,
His age will brighten as his years decline.

M.A.F.

Title Pages Of Contemporary Books
Relating To Mrs Fraser

NARRATIVE

OF THE

CAPTURE, SUFFERINGS, AND MIRACULOUS ESCAPE

OF

MRS. ELIZA FRASER,

Wife of the late Captain SAMUEL FRASER, commander of the ship *Sterling Castle*, which was wrecked on 25th May, in latitude 34, and longitude 155, 12, east, on Eliza Reef, on her passage from New South Wales to Liverpool—a part of the crew having taken to the long boat, were driven to and thrown on an unknown island, inhabited by Savages, by whom Captain Fraser and his first mate were barbarously murdered, and Mrs. Fraser (the wife of the former, with the 2d mate and steward) were for several weeks held in bondage, and after having been compelled to take up her abode in a wigwam and to become the adopted wife of one of the Chiefs, Mrs. F. was providentially rescued from her perilous situation.

An Indian Chief in the act of forcibly conveying Mrs. Fraser to his hut or wigwam.

NEW-YORK:
PUBLISHED BY CHARLES S. WEBB.---1837.

TALES OF TRAVELLERS;

OR,

A VIEW OF THE WORLD.

No 48.] SATURDAY, SEPTEMBER 2, 1837. [PRICE 1*d*.

WRECK OF THE STIRLING CASTLE.

[THE MURDER OF THE CAPTAIN.]

On the 16th of May, 1835, the *Stirling Castle* left Sydney for the purpose of going to Singapore. On the 23d, when they were approaching Torres Straits, it blew very fresh, and there being a current near the Eliza coral reefs, which the vessel was unable to resist, she struck on the reefs at about nine o'clock at night, when the captain was incapable, on account of the hazy weather, of making observations. There were about eighteen men on board, two boys, and Mrs. Frazer, the captain's wife, who was far advanced in pregnancy. Two of the men, who were labouring at the wheel, were killed when the ship struck, and the cabins were dashed into the hold, together with all the bread, beef, pork, and other provisions. The crew, when the tempest ceased, contrived to cut away the masts, in the expectation that, with the assistance of the tide, the ship would right herself; and she did in some degree change her position, but not to any serviceable extent. They, therefore, determined to get away as well as they could in the long-boat and the pinnace, which they had contrived to keep secure, the two other boats which were attached to the ship having been swept away by the fury of the elements. They knew that they were to the northward of Moreton Bay, a portion of the settlements of the English crown, and they determined to make for that place with as much expedition as possible. Accordingly, having worked with most desperate industry until four o'clock on Sunday, they disembarked from the vessel, and took to the boats. The ship's

SHIPWRECK

OF THE

STIRLING CASTLE,

CONTAINING

A FAITHFUL NARRATIVE OF THE DREADFUL SUFFERINGS OF THE CREW,

AND THE

CRUEL MURDER OF CAPTAIN FRASER

BY THE SAVAGES.

ALSO,

THE HORRIBLE BARBARITY OF THE CANNIBALS INFLICTED UPON

THE CAPTAIN'S WIDOW,

WHOSE UNPARALLELED SUFFERINGS ARE STATED BY HERSELF, AND
CORROBORATED BY THE OTHER SURVIVORS.

TO WHICH IS ADDED,

THE NARRATIVE OF THE WRECK OF THE

CHARLES EATON,

IN THE SAME LATITUDE.

Embellished with Engravings, Portraits, and Scenes illustrative of the Narrative.

By JOHN CURTIS.

LONDON:

PUBLISHED BY GEORGE VIRTUE, IVY LANE,

AND SOLD BY ALL BOOKSELLERS.

M.DCCC.XXXVIII.

THE

SHIPWRECK OF MRS. FRAZER,

AND

LOSS OF THE STIRLING CASTLE,

ON A CORAL REEF IN THE SOUTH PACIFIC OCEAN.

CONTAINING AN ACCOUNT OF THE

HITHERTO-UNHEARD-OF SUFFERINGS AND HARDSHIPS OF THE CREW,
WHO EXISTED SEVEN DAYS WITHOUT FOOD OR WATER.

THE DREADFUL

SUFFERINGS OF MRS. FRAZER,

WHO, WITH HER HUSBAND, AND THE SURVIVORS OF THE ILL-FATED
CREW, ARE

CAPTURED BY THE SAVAGES OF NEW HOLLAND,

AND BY THEM STRIPPED ENTIRELY NAKED, AND DRIVEN INTO THE
BUSH.

THEIR DREADFUL SLAVERY, CRUEL TOIL, AND EXCRUCIATING
TORTURES INFLICTED ON THEM.

THE HORRID DEATH OF Mr. BROWN,

WHO WAS ROASTED ALIVE OVER A SLOW FIRE KINDLED BENEATH HIS FEET!

MEETING OF MR. AND MRS. FRAZER, AND

INHUMAN MURDER OF CAPTAIN FRAZER

IN THE PRESENCE OF HIS WIFE,

BARBAROUS TREATMENT OF MRS. FRAZER, WHO IS TORTURED,
SPEARED, AND WOUNDED BY THE SAVAGES.

THE FORTUNATE ESCAPE OF ONE OF THE CREW,

TO MORETON BAY, A NEIGHBOURING BRITISH SETTLEMENT,

BY WHOSE INSTRUMENTALITY, THROUGH THE INGENUITY OF A CONVICT, NAMED
GRAHAM, THE SURVIVORS OBTAIN THEIR

DELIVERANCE FROM THE SAVAGES.

THEIR SUBSEQUENT ARRIVAL IN ENGLAND, AND APPEARANCE BEFORE THE LORD
MAYOR OF LONDON,

INTERSPERSED WITH THE

SUFFERINGS AND ADVENTURES OF ROBERT DARG, ONE OF THE CREW.

LONDON:

PUBLISHED BY DEAN AND MUNDAY, THREADNEEDLE-STREET.

Price Sixpence.